Presented to:

꧁꧂꧁꧂꧁꧂꧁꧂꧁꧂꧁꧂꧁꧂꧁꧂꧁꧂

From:

꧁꧂꧁꧂꧁꧂꧁꧂꧁꧂꧁꧂꧁꧂꧁꧂꧁꧂

FOOTSTEPS TO FOLLOW

Eternal Truths for Christian Living

Dr. Edward Pauley

A J. Countryman Book
Book design by Kandi Shepherd

ISBN: 0-8499-5364-2 (hardcover)
ISBN: 0-8499-5365-0 (softcover)

Printed and bound in the United States of America
8 9 0 1 2 3 4 RRD 9 8 7 6 5 4 3 2 1

CONTENTS

〰〰〰

Truth

The Bible

God

Jesus Christ

〰〰〰

Contents

The Holy Spirit

Angels

Satan and Demons

Mankind

Sin

Contents

Salvation

Discipleship

Stewardship

Relationships

The Church

Contents

TRUTH

We are of God. He who knows God hears us; he who is not of God does not hear us. By this we know the spirit of truth and the spirit of error.

1 John 4:6

Pilate therefore said to Him, "Are You a king then?" Jesus answered, "You say rightly that I am a king. For this cause I was born, and for this cause I have come into the world, that I should bear witness to the truth. Everyone who is of the truth hears My voice."

John 18:37

Pilate said to Him, "What is truth?" And when he had said this, he went out again to the Jews, and said to them, "I find no fault in Him at all."

John 18:38

But they have not all obeyed the gospel. For Isaiah says, "Lord, who has believed our report?" So then faith comes by hearing, and hearing by the word of God.

Romans 10:16–17

For what if some did not believe? Will their unbelief make the faithfulness of God without effect? Certainly not! Indeed, let God be true but every man a liar.

Romans 3:3–4a

WHEN PILATE ASKED "What is truth?" he was being skeptical and cynical. Many people today doubt objective truth, ascribing all truth claims to selfish or group-centered motives. But the Bible clearly teaches that God has revealed truth that is true whether anyone knows it or believes it. Objective facts make a claim true, not personal opinion. It is the Holy Spirit who persuades someone that the gospel is true, granting faith to believe its claims.

Application: Christians can have confidence that their faith is grounded in facts, not feelings.

Response: *Father, thank You for showing me that Your Word is true, and that I may stake my eternal destiny upon it.*

The entirety of Your word is truth, And every one of Your righteous judgments endures forever.

Psalm 119:160

Or is He the God of the Jews only? Is He not also the God of the Gentiles? Yes, of the Gentiles also.

Romans 3:29

Who desires all men to be saved and to come to the knowledge of the truth. For there is one God and one Mediator between God and men, the Man Christ Jesus.

1 Timothy 2:4–5

For the grace of God that brings salvation has appeared to all men.

Titus 2:11

Truly, these times of ignorance God overlooked, but now commands all men everywhere to repent, because He has appointed a day on which He will judge the world in righteousness by the Man whom He has ordained. He has given assurance of this to all by raising Him from the dead.

Acts 17:30–31

I F ANYTHING IS TRUE, it is true always, everywhere, and for everyone. The message of the Bible is not for one nation or one culture or one age but for every nation, every culture, and every age. That is why Jesus commanded His disciples to carry the message of the gospel to the entire world and to call on everyone to repent and trust Him alone for salvation. There is not one truth for you and a different truth for me. There is only one truth for everyone.

Application: It does not matter what the personal or cultural background of an individual may be. The truth of the gospel of repentance and faith in Christ for the forgiveness of sins applies to everyone alike.

Response: O Lord, help me to have confidence that when I share the gospel with someone from another culture, it applies to that person just as truly as it applies to me.

He is the Rock, His work is perfect;
For all His ways are justice.
A God of truth and without injustice;
Righteous and upright is He.

Deuteronomy 32:4

But the LORD is the true God;
He is the living God and the everlasting King.

Jeremiah 10:10a

And this is eternal life, that they may know You, the only true God, and Jesus Christ whom You have sent.

John 17:3

Jesus said to him, "I am . . . the truth. . . ."

John 14:6

ALL TRUTH IS ROOTED in the person and character of God. He embodies truth. He personifies truth. He is truth. God's Word is true, and His commandments are true, because He is true. To say God is true is to say that He is totally trustworthy and faithful. It is also to say that He is totally honest and will never lie. Finally, it is to say that He is totally real and good. He defines what reality and goodness are since He created and exemplifies them. He is the God of truth, and no one else is.

Application: If people want to know what truth is, they only have to look into the face of Jesus Christ.

Response: Lord Jesus, since You are the very embodiment of truth, I acknowledge You as the standard of everything I must live by and become.

And you shall know the truth, and the truth shall make you free.

John 8:32

∽∽∽∽∽

That if you confess with your mouth the Lord Jesus and believe in your heart that God has raised Him from the dead, you will be saved.

Romans 10:9

∽∽∽∽∽

Therefore I will not be negligent to remind you always of these things, though you know them, and are established in the present truth.

2 Peter 1:12

∽∽∽∽∽

These things I have written to you who believe in the name of the Son of God, that you may know that you have eternal life, and that you may continue to believe in the name of the Son of God.

1 John 5:13

> But without faith it is impossible to please Him, for he who comes to God must believe that He is, and that He is a rewarder of those who diligently seek Him.
>
> *Hebrews 11:6*

CHRISTIANITY IS DISTINCTIVE from other religions in one major respect: It claims that the Bible reveals truths, or propositions, that may be known and believed. In fact, the Bible reveals truths that must be believed and acted upon if a person is to have eternal life. While unaided reason is not sufficient by itself to understand these truths, the illumination provided by the Holy Spirit helps us to understand and believe the truth of the gospel. God has made us rational creatures like Himself and has chosen to use the medium of language to communicate in His Word truths that we can and must know.

Application: Believers do not have to turn off their minds but are able to know individual truths that God has revealed in Scripture.

Response: Heavenly Father, how grateful I am that I can worship You with all of my mind as well as all of my heart.

If you know these things, happy are you if you do them.

John 13:17

∽∽∽∽∽

You ran well. Who hindered you from obeying the truth?

Galatians 5:7

∽∽∽∽∽

The things which you learned and received and heard and saw in me, these do, and the God of peace will be with you.

Philippians 4:9

∽∽∽∽∽

If we say that we have fellowship with Him, and walk in darkness, we lie and do not practice the truth.

1 John 1:6

But he who does the truth comes to the light, that his deeds may be clearly seen, that they have been done in God.

John 3:21

THE BIBLE SPEAKS of God's commandments as well as His statements as being truth. Whereas God's statements are to be believed, His commandments are to be obeyed. This is called "doing the truth" and is the same thing as abiding in Christ or walking according to the Spirit. It is the Christian life as God designed it. We do the truth because we believe the truth and have trusted Him who is the truth. For this reason, if our lives do not match our profession of faith, the genuineness of our claim to believe the truth of the gospel may be called into question.

Application: A head knowledge of the gospel that does not translate into a Christlike life is a merely intellectual understanding of God's truth and will not save anyone.

Response: Lord Jesus, I cannot call you Lord unless I do the things you say. Because You are my Lord, I desire to obey You.

THE BIBLE

God, who at various times and in different ways spoke in time past to the fathers by the prophets, has in these last days spoken to us by His Son. . . .

Hebrews 1:1–2

At that time Jesus answered and said, "I thank You, Father, Lord of heaven and earth, because You have hidden these things from the wise and prudent and have revealed them to babes."

Matthew 11:25

And the Word became flesh and dwelt among us, and we beheld His glory, the glory as of the only begotten of the Father, full of grace and truth. . . . No one has seen God at any time. The only begotten Son, who is in the bosom of the Father, He has declared Him.

John 1:14, 18

For I have given to them the words which You have given Me; and they have received them, and have known surely that I came forth from You; and they have believed that You sent Me.

John 17:8

> The secret things belong to the LORD our God, but those things which are revealed belong to us and to our children forever, that we may do all the words of this law.
>
> *Deuteronomy 29:29*

SOME THINGS MAY be known by observation. Other things, especially about other people, may only be known if those individuals choose to open up and tell us about themselves. God is a person and has chosen to disclose some of His thoughts, feelings, and actions through the medium of language in His Word, the Bible. We may know some things about God by observing the world He has created. But we know the most important things, especially who He is and what He wants, because He has revealed them in His Word.

Application: God has shared with us in the Bible all the things we need to know about Him and His will for us. We never have to look elsewhere for wisdom.

Response: O Lord, I come to You as a hungry child, seeking the nourishment of Your Word.

Then the LORD said to Moses, "Write these words, for according to the tenor of these words I have made a covenant with you and with Israel."

Exodus 34:27

The word that came to Jeremiah from the LORD, saying, "Thus speaks the LORD God of Israel, saying: 'Write in a book for yourself all the words that I have spoken to you.'"

Jeremiah 30:1–2

These things we also speak, not in words which man's wisdom teaches but which the Holy Spirit teaches, comparing spiritual things with spiritual.

1 Corinthians 2:13

Knowing this first, that no prophecy of Scripture is of any private interpretation, for prophecy never came by the will of man, but holy men of God spoke as they were moved by the Holy Spirit.

2 Peter 1:20–21

All Scripture is given by inspiration of God, and is profitable for doctrine, for reproof, for correction, for instruction in righteousness.

2 Timothy 3:16

THE BIBLE IS GOD'S written Word. Prophets and apostles were moved by the Holy Spirit to write exactly what God wanted them to write. In some cases, the words they spoke and wrote were dictated by God. In every case, their own personalities and life experiences were used by God, and they shine through the text. Sometimes the writers understood what they were writing, and sometimes they did not. But always they wrote in obedience to the prompting of the Holy Spirit. The process by which the Holy Spirit led them to write is called inspiration, a word that means God-breathed.

Application: When we open the Bible, we are reading words that were written by human beings under the influence and control of the Holy Spirit. We should consider those words, taken together, to be the very words of God.

Response: *Heavenly Father, I hear Your voice speaking to my heart and mind as I read Your Word, the Bible.*

God is not a man, that He should lie, nor a son of man, that He should repent. Has He said, and will He not do it? Or has He spoken, and will He not make it good?

Numbers 23:19

For assuredly, I say to you, till heaven and earth pass away, one jot or one tittle will by no means pass from the law till all is fulfilled.

Matthew 5:18

Having been born again, not of corruptible seed but incorruptible, through the word of God which lives and abides forever, . . . but the word of the LORD endures forever.

1 Peter 1:23, 25

Sanctify them by Your truth. Your word is truth.

John 17:17

EVERYTHING THAT IS stated in the Bible is true and free from error. The prophets and apostles were preserved by the Holy Spirit from making any mistakes when they wrote the original Hebrew and Greek texts of the Bible. While we do not have the original manuscripts, we have thousands of ancient copies that agree with one another to a remarkably high degree—so much so that we may have confidence that the texts we have are indeed the inspired, inerrant Word of God. We should expect God to communicate only truth since He embodies truth and cannot lie.

Application: For the Christian, the Bible is the ultimate authority on every matter it addresses since all its claims are true. It is the absolute standard for everything a Christian believes or does.

Response: *Oh Lord, I praise you for giving me a totally reliable guide for faith and living in Your holy Word, the Bible.*

It is written in the prophets, "And they shall all be taught by God." Therefore everyone who has heard and learned from the Father comes to Me.

John 6:45

But the Helper, the Holy Spirit, whom the Father will send in My name, He will teach you all things, and bring to your remembrance all things that I said to you.

John 14:26

However, when He, the Spirit of truth, has come, He will guide you into all truth; for He will not speak on His own authority, but whatever He hears He will speak; and He will tell you things to come.

John 16:13

Now we have received, not the spirit of the world, but the Spirit who is from God, that we might know the things that have been freely given to us by God. These things we also speak not in words which man's wisdom teaches but which the Holy Spirit teaches, comparing spiritual things with spiritual.

1 Corinthians 2:12–13

But the natural man does not receive the things of the Spirit of God, for they are foolishness to him; nor can he know them, because they are spiritually discerned.

1 Corinthians 2:14

WHILE THE BIBLE IS a rational book whose claims are all true, it is at the same time a spiritual book whose claims will be believed only by those whose minds are illumined by the Holy Spirit. Reason is necessary to understand the claims of the Bible, but reason is not sufficient to be convinced of its truth. For that to occur, the person reading it must be persuaded by the Holy Spirit living within, which means the reader must believe in the Lord Jesus Christ. During Christ's earthly ministry, He told His disciples He would send the Holy Spirit to live inside believers to teach and remind them of the truth of God's Word.

Application: The only way for us understand what the Bible says is to receive the illumination that the Holy Spirit provides, that is, to have the Holy Spirit as our Teacher.

Response: Spirit of God, I ask You to convict me of the truth of the Bible as I read it, and show me how it applies to my life. Be my Teacher today.

All the ends of the world shall remember and turn to the LORD and all the families of the nations shall worship before You.

Psalm 22:27

I keep Your precepts and Your testimonies, For all my ways are before You.

Psalm 119:168

Thus says the LORD of hosts, "In those days ten men from every language of the nations shall grasp the sleeve of a Jewish man, saying, 'Let us go with you, for we have heard that God is with you.'"

Zechariah 8:23

Then I saw another angel flying in the midst of heaven, having the everlasting gospel to preach to those who dwell on the earth—to every nation, tribe, tongue, and people.

Revelation 14:6

THE BIBLE SPEAKS to every area of our lives. It has principles that are relevant to everything we think, say, and do. It is truly a blueprint for Christian living. It is also applicable to everything we learn as well as to every calling in life. It is relevant to every age, people, and culture. Its truths can be formulated in every human language and applied to every social group. It has a timeless, universal message that fits the human condition. This is because the One who gave this revelation to humankind is the One who created humanity in the first place and who knows everything about us.

Application: The Bible's principles apply to all people, no matter what group they belong to. These principles cross all cultural boundaries and apply to every situation in life.

Response: Heavenly Father, how grateful I am that I can find the wisdom I need in Your Word. You always have a word that fits my circumstance.

GOD

Hear, O Israel: The LORD our God, the LORD is one!

Deuteronomy 6:4

Now I am no longer in the world, but these are in the world, and I come to You. Holy Father, keep through Your name those whom You have given Me, that they may be one as We are. . . . And the glory which You gave Me I have given them, that they may be one just as We are one: I in them, and You in Me; that they may be made perfect in one, and that the world may know that You have sent Me, and have loved them as You have loved Me.

John 17:11, 22–23

For there is one God and one Mediator between God and men, the Man Christ Jesus.

1 Timothy 2:5

I do not pray for these alone, but also for those who will believe in Me through their word; that they all may be one, as You, Father, are in Me, and I in You; that they also may be one in Us, that the world may believe that You sent Me.

John 17:20–21

CHRISTIANS BELIEVE in only one God. But the God they worship has revealed Himself to be a complex unity. He is a single being consisting of three persons: the Father, the Son, and the Holy Spirit. These three have intimate fellowship with one another in a perfect union. In a similar way, we are invited into an intimate personal relationship with the triune God, not into the union of the godhead but into unity with the godhead.

Application: The intimate, harmonious relationship of the three Persons of the Godhead is a perfect model for the unity of Christians who make up the body of Christ.

Response: *Heavenly Father, help me to show love to my brothers and sisters in Christ so others may be drawn to You.*

Then God said, "Let Us make man in Our image, according to Our likeness; let them have dominion over the fish of the sea, over the birds of the air, and over the cattle, over all the earth and over every creeping thing that creeps on the earth."

Genesis 1:26

And I will pray the Father, and He will give you another Helper, that He may abide with you forever. . . . Jesus answered and said to him, "If anyone loves Me, he will keep My word; and My Father will love him, and We will come to him and make Our home with him."

John 14:16, 23

The grace of the Lord Jesus Christ, and the love of God, and the communion of the Holy Spirit be with you all. Amen.

2 Corinthians 13:14

For through Him we both have access by one Spirit to the Father.

Ephesians 2:18

Go therefore and make disciples of all the nations, baptizing them in the name of the Father, and of the Son and of the Holy Spirit.

Matthew 28:19

HUMAN BEINGS AND ANGELS are one-person beings; each one is a single individual. By contrast, God is a three-person being: the Father, the Son, and the Holy Spirit. Because all three persons of the Trinity are equally God, each has all the attributes of God. They differ only in role. The Father is the author of salvation, the Son is the agent or means of salvation, and the Holy Spirit implements God's plan of salvation. That is why Christians are baptized in the name of all three persons of the Godhead.

Application: The plurality of Persons in the Godhead is reflected in the plurality of aspects of each human being: the mind, the will, and the emotions.

Response: O Lord, how incredible it is to realize I have been created in the image of a triune God, that my complexity mirrors Yours!

As a father pities his children, so the LORD pities those who fear Him.

Psalm 103:13

You, O LORD, are our Father; Our Redeemer from Everlasting is Your name.

Isaiah 63:16

For this reason I bow my knees to the Father of our Lord Jesus Christ, from whom the whole family in heaven and earth is named.

Ephesians 3:14–15

Blessed be the God and Father of our Lord Jesus Christ, who according to His abundant mercy has begotten us again to a living hope through the resurrection of Jesus Christ from the dead.

1 Peter 1:3

In this manner, therefore, pray: Our Father in heaven, hallowed be Your name. Your kingdom come. Your will be done on earth as it is in heaven.

Matthew 6:9–10

G OD THE FATHER is the executive member of the godhead. He is the architect of creation and the devisor of the plan of salvation. In the counsels of the godhead, He is first among equals, and it is His will that is carried out by the Son and the Holy Spirit. Therefore, it is to Him that Christians pray in the name of the Son and in the power of the Holy Spirit.

Application: All believers have a Father in heaven. Because God is our Father, we have a family relationship to Him and to one another.

Response: Almighty God, what a joy it is to call You Father and to know You love me as Your child!

For unto us a Child is born, unto us a Son is given; and the government will be upon His shoulder and His name will be called Wonderful, Counselor, Mighty God, Everlasting Father, Prince of Peace.

Isaiah 9:6

Then Jesus came and spoke to them, saying, "All authority has been given to Me in heaven and on earth."

Matthew 28:18

For God did not send His Son into the World to condemn the world, but that the world through Him might be saved.

John 3:17

For I have come down from heaven, not to do My own will, but the will of Him who sent Me.

John 6:38

I will declare the decree: The LORD has said to Me, "You are My Son, today I have begotten You."

Psalm 2:7

GOD THE SON is the second person of the Trinity. He is the primary agent for carrying out the Father's will, both in creation and in salvation. As the Son of God in whom the Father has vested all authority in heaven and on earth, He is to be worshiped and His will obeyed. Through the person of the Holy Spirit, Jesus Christ comes to live and reign in the hearts of believers.

Application: For the Christian, the Son of God is the bridge between earth and heaven. He covers our sins and brings us home to the Father.

Response: Lord Jesus, I cannot fully understand why You stooped to save Your own creation, but I am eternally grateful that You did.

But the Helper, the Holy Spirit, whom the Father will send in My name, He will teach you all things, and bring to your remembrance all things that I said to you.

John 14:26

When He, the Spirit of truth, has come, He will guide you into all truth; for He will not speak on His own authority, but whatever He hears He will speak; and He will tell you things to come. He will glorify Me, for He will take of what is Mine and declare it to you.

John 16:13–14

Or do you not know that your body is the temple of the Holy Spirit who is in you, whom you have from God, and you are not your own?

1 Corinthians 6:19

For by one Spirit we were all baptized into one body— whether Jews or Greeks, whether slaves or free—and have all been made to drink into one Spirit.

1 Corinthians 12:13

But when the Helper comes, whom I shall send to you from the Father, the Spirit of truth who proceeds from the Father, He will testify of Me.

John 15:26

GOD THE HOLY SPIRIT is the third person of the Trinity. He carries out the will of both the Father and the Son. His role is to point us to the Son and to make us over into the image of the Son. As the Son is eternally begotten of the Father, so the Holy Spirit eternally proceeds from and is sent by both the Father and the Son. His presence in our hearts regenerates us spiritually and imparts the grace, truth, and power of God to our lives.

Application: As the Son brings us to the Father, so the Spirit brings the Father and the Son to us. For this reason, the entire Godhead indwells the believer.

Response: Spirit of God, because You have made my body Your temple, I want to live to honor You, not to grieve You.

JESUS CHRIST

And the Word became flesh and dwelt among us, and we beheld His glory, the glory as of the only begotten of the Father, full of grace and truth.

John 1:14

Concerning His Son Jesus Christ our Lord, who was born of the seed of David according to the flesh, and declared to be the Son of God with power, according to the Spirit of holiness, by the resurrection from the dead.

Romans 1:3–4

Of whom are the fathers and from whom, according to the flesh, Christ came, who is over all, the eternally blessed God. Amen.

Romans 9:5

But when the fullness of the time had come, God sent forth His Son, born of a woman, born under the law.

Galatians 4:4

> [Christ] Who committed no sin, . . . who Himself bore our sins
> in His own body on the tree. . . .
>
> *1 Peter 2:22, 24*

WHEN JESUS CHRIST, the eternal Son of God, became the Son of Man by being born of Mary, He took on a physical body (the incarnation), thereby receiving a second human nature that was joined to His divine nature. This made Him one person with two natures: the God-man. Both natures were complete: neither one was diminished by the other. Because Jesus is completely God, He could pay the penalty for all of our sins. Because He was completely man, He was capable of dying on the cross. As man, He could experience everything we experience; as God, He could do so without sinning.

Application: Jesus is not a distant God who cannot understand our human condition, but One who both understands our frailty and gives us power to overcome it.

Response: Lord Jesus, You faced the same temptations I face, and I know your power is sufficient to help me be victorious.

Therefore the Lord Himself will give you a sign: Behold, the virgin shall conceive and bear a Son, and shall call His name Immanuel.

Isaiah 7:14

⬡⬡⬡

Now the birth of Jesus Christ was as follows: After His mother Mary was betrothed to Joseph, before they came together, she was found with child of the Holy Spirit.

Matthew 1:18

⬡⬡⬡

But while he thought about these things, behold, an angel of the Lord appeared to him in a dream, saying, "Joseph, son of David, do not be afraid to take to you Mary your wife, for that which is conceived in her is of the Holy Spirit."

Matthew 1:20

⬡⬡⬡

Then Mary said to the angel, "How can this be, since I do not know a man?"

Luke 1:34

⬡⬡⬡

But when the fullness of the time had come, God sent forth His Son, born of a woman, born under the law.

Galatians 4:4

⬡⬡⬡

The Holy Spirit will come upon you, and the power of the Highest will overshadow you; therefore, also, that Holy One who is to be born will be called the Son of God.

Luke 1:35

JESUS' VIRGIN BIRTH is significant to His status as the Son of God and to His sinlessness. To say that Jesus was born of a virgin is to say more than that His conception was directly and miraculously caused by God the Father through the Holy Spirit without the agency of a human father. It is to say that Jesus is the Son of God in an absolutely unique sense, that He is the only one begotten rather than made by the Father and that He is free of the sin that has infected the rest of humanity.

Application: Because Jesus was not polluted by Adam's sin, He was able to die for the sins of everyone else. If He had not been born of a virgin, we would not have had a perfect Savior.

Response: Lord Jesus, how grateful I am that you are the holy Son of God who alone could pay the penalty my sins deserve.

But He was wounded for our transgressions, He was bruised for our iniquities; the chastisement for our peace was upon Him, and by His stripes we are healed.

Isaiah 53:5

Whom God set forth to be a propitiation by His blood, through faith, to demonstrate His righteousness, because in His forbearance God had passed over the sins that were previously committed.

Romans 3:25

So Christ was offered once to bear the sins of many. To those who eagerly wait for Him He will appear a second time apart from sin, for salvation.

Hebrews 9:28

By that will we have been sanctified through the offering of the body of Jesus Christ once for all.

Hebrews 10:10

God was in Christ reconciling the world to Himself, not imputing their trespasses to them, . . . for He made Him who knew no sin to be sin for us, that we might become the righteousness of God in Him.

2 Corinthians 5:19, 21

JESUS CHRIST IS THE only one who ever came into the world to die. His death on the cross to pay the penalty we owed for our sins satisfied the Father's justice and expressed the Father's love. Jesus' death in our place, as our substitute, not only covered our sins but reconciled us to the Father. Jesus' blood, representing His life given for us, continues to cleanse us from all sin and restore our fellowship with the Father. By believing that He was the sacrifice for our sins, we are declared forgiven and righteous enough to enter heaven.

Application: Christians get the best bargain in the universe. They get to swap their sins for Christ's righteousness because Christ swapped His life for theirs.

Response: Heavenly Father, I come to You once again pleading the blood of Jesus as my only defense and my one hope of forgiveness and cleansing.

That if you confess with your mouth the Lord Jesus and believe in your heart that God has raised Him from the dead, you will be saved.

Romans 10:9

And if Christ is not risen, then our preaching is vain and your faith is also vain. . . . But now Christ is risen from the dead, and has become the first fruits of those who have fallen asleep.

1 Corinthians 15:14, 20

That I may know Him and the power of His resurrection, and the fellowship of His sufferings, being conformed to His death, if, by any means, I may attain to the resurrection from the dead.

Philippians 3:10–11

[This is the gospel of God] concerning His Son Jesus Christ our Lord, who was born of the seed of David according to the flesh, and declared to be the Son of God with power according to the Spirit of holiness, by the resurrection from the dead.

Romans 1:3–4

OTHER THAN THE incarnation, the most significant historical event in the life of Jesus Christ on this earth was His resurrection. On the third day after His crucifixion for our sins, Jesus rose bodily from the dead in the same body in which He had died and was buried, but one transformed in every respect into a body fit for heaven. Because of His resurrection, we know He is the Son of God and that His sacrifice of Himself was acceptable to the Father.

Application: Because Jesus Christ is alive, really alive, we who believe in Him shall also live and have resurrection bodies like His when He returns for His own.

Response: Lord Jesus, I know this life is not all there is because You came back to life from death to show there is victory over death and the grave.

Therefore you also be ready, for the Son of Man is coming at an hour when you do not expect Him.

Matthew 24:44

Men of Galilee, why do you stand gazing up into heaven? This same Jesus who was taken up from you into heaven, will so come in like manner as you saw Him go into heaven.

Acts 1:11

When Christ who is our life appears, then you also will appear with Him in glory.

Colossians 3:4

For the Lord Himself will descend from heaven with a shout, with the voice of an archangel, and with the trumpet of God. And the dead in Christ will rise first. Then we who are alive and remain shall be caught up together with them in the clouds to meet the Lord in the air. And thus we shall always be with the Lord.

1 Thessalonians 4:16–17

Looking for the blessed hope and glorious appearing of our great God and Savior Jesus Christ.

Titus 2:13

THE BLESSED HOPE of all Christians is the return of Jesus Christ to this world in great power and glory. When the trumpet sounds and He appears, every eye shall see Him as He breaks through the sky accompanied by the holy angels and the spirits of those who have died as believers. He will descend to the Mount of Olives outside Jerusalem where He ascended forty days after His resurrection. The first time Jesus came to seek and save the lost; the second time He will come to judge and to reign. For the Christian, Christ's Second Coming will be a source of joy; for the unbeliever, it will be a source of terror. For believers, it is important to be ready when He comes, to live holy lives so we will not be ashamed at His coming.

Application: The thought that Jesus could appear at any moment should be the greatest motivation the Christian has for holy living.

Response: *With John I say, "Even so, come, Lord Jesus!"*

THE HOLY SPIRIT

For as many as are led by the Spirit of God, these are sons of God. . . . The Spirit Himself bears witness with our spirit that we are children of God.

Romans 8:14, 16

Likewise the Spirit also helps in our weaknesses. For we do not know what we should pray for as we ought, but the Spirit Himself makes intercession for us with groanings which cannot be uttered. Now He who searches the hearts knows what the mind of the Spirit is, because He makes intercession for the saints according to the will of God.

Romans 8:26–27

Now the Lord is the Spirit; and where the Spirit of the Lord is, there is liberty. But we all, with unveiled face, beholding as in a mirror the glory of the Lord, are being transformed into the same image from glory to glory, just as by the Spirit of the Lord.

2 Corinthians 3:17–18

And do not grieve the Holy Spirit of God, by whom you were sealed for the day of redemption.

Ephesians 4:30

> But Peter said, "Ananias, why has Satan filled your heart to lie to
> the Holy Spirit . . . ? You have not lied to men but to God."
>
> *Acts 5:3–4*

THE HOLY SPIRIT is the third person of the Trinity. He is God—
coequal, coexistent, and coeternal with the Father and the Son. As
a person, He has a mind, a will, and feelings. He can be lied to and
grieved. He can pray, speak, teach, remind, and lead. Only a person can
do all of these things. When the Holy Spirit enters a human spirit, he
makes it come alive from the death of sin into a new life in Christ.

Application: As Christians, we have a divine Person living inside of us.
Because the Holy Spirit is one with the Father and the Son, we there-
fore have the entire Godhead living inside of us through the Holy
Spirit.

*Response: Heavenly Father, may I be obedient to the voice of the Spirit as
He speaks to me through Your Word.*

I indeed baptize you with water unto repentance, but He who is coming after me is mightier than I, whose sandals I am not worthy to carry. He will baptize you with the Holy Spirit and fire.

Matthew 3:11

But as many as received Him, to them He gave the right to become children of God, even to those who believe in His name: Who were born, not of blood, nor of the will of the flesh, nor of the will of man, but of God.

John 1:12–13

Jesus answered, "Most assuredly, I say to you, unless one is born of water and the Spirit, he cannot enter the kingdom of God. That which is born of the flesh is flesh, and that which is born of the Spirit is spirit."

John 3:5–6

But you are not in the flesh but in the Spirit, if indeed the Spirit of God dwells in you. Now if anyone does not have the Spirit of Christ, he is not His.

Romans 8:9

> For by one Spirit we were all baptized into one body—whether
> Jews or Greeks, whether slaves or free—and have all been made
> to drink into one Spirit.
>
> *1 Corinthians 12:13*

THE MOMENT A PERSON receives Jesus Christ as Savior and Lord, the Holy Spirit comes into that person's heart and takes up permanent residence. That happens only once in the life of the believer. To be indwelt by the Spirit is to be reborn spiritually. Just as natural birth occurs only once, so spiritual birth occurs only once. There are many fillings of the Spirit in the life of the believer, but only one baptism of the Spirit. When we are baptized with the Holy Spirit, we are united both to Jesus Christ and to His body, the church.

Application: Water baptism cannot take away sin; Spirit baptism cleanses us from all sin and makes us brand new persons.

Response: Lord Jesus, thank You for coming into my heart and for sending Your Spirit to live there forever.

And the disciples were filled with joy and with the Holy Spirit.

Acts 13:52

For as many as are led by the Spirit of God, these are sons of God.

Romans 8:14

I say then: Walk in the Spirit, and you shall not fulfill the lust of the flesh.

Galatians 5:16

And those who are Christ's have crucified the flesh with its passions and desires. If we live in the Spirit, let us also walk in the Spirit.

Galatians 5:24–25

> And do not be drunk with wine, in which is dissipation; but be filled with the Spirit.
>
> *Ephesians 5:18*

WHEN WE CONFESS all known sin and yield the control of our lives to the Lord Jesus Christ, we are filled by the Holy Spirit. Yielding to the Lordship of Christ and to the control of the Spirit are one and the same thing. Christ lives in our hearts when the Holy Spirit takes up residence; He becomes Lord of our lives when the Holy Spirit is in control. Because we are still in the flesh, we all too often take back the control of our lives and the Holy Spirit then no longer fills us. That is why we are commanded to be continually filled with the Holy Spirit.

Application: We must keep short accounts with God if we are to walk in the fullness of the Holy Spirit.

Response: Lord Jesus, cleanse me and fill me with Your Holy Spirit once again.

Therefore by their fruits you will know them.

Matthew 7:20

❦

I am the vine, you are the branches. He who abides in Me, and I in him, bears much fruit; for without Me you can do nothing.

John 15:5

❦

You did not choose Me, but I chose you and appointed you that you should go and bear fruit, and that your fruit should remain, that whatever you ask the Father in My name He may give you.

John 15:16

❦

For the fruit of the Spirit is in all goodness, righteousness, and truth.

Ephesians 5:9

But the fruit of the Spirit is love, joy, peace, longsuffering, kindness, goodness, faithfulness, gentleness, self-control. Against such there is no law.

Galatians 5:22–23

SOMETHING HAPPENS to us and through us when we abide in Christ, when we are filled with the Spirit. We bear fruit. This "fruit" is the collection of attitudes, actions, and character traits that were exemplified in the life of Jesus and that increasingly become ours as the Holy Spirit transforms our attitudes, actions, and character. We not only take on the character traits of Jesus but we act like Jesus. The fruits of the Spirit will be evident to others both in our attitudes and in our actions.

Application: Just as bearing fruit is the sign of life in a tree, so having the attitude and characteristics of Jesus are signs of His life and Lordship in our lives.

Response: O Father, how I long for the world to see that Jesus lives and rules in my life!

Having then gifts differing according to the grace that is given to us, let us use them.

Romans 12:6

Now there are diversities of gifts, but the same Spirit. . . . But the manifestation of the Spirit is given to each one for the profit of all.

1 Corinthians 12:4, 7

But one and the same Spirit works all these things, distributing to each one individually as He wills.

1 Corinthians 12:11

As each one has received a gift, minister it to one another, as good stewards of the manifold grace of God.

1 Peter 4:10

And He Himself gave some to be apostles, some prophets, some evangelists, and some pastors and teachers, for the equipping of the saints for the work of the ministry, for the edifying of the body of Christ.

Ephesians 4:11–12

BELIEVERS ENCOURAGE other believers by exercising the gifts of the Holy Spirit. These gifts are abilities that are given to different individuals in accordance with the sovereign will of the Spirit at the time they become Christians. Spiritual gifts are different from natural talents, which belong to both believers and nonbelievers. Only Christians have spiritual gifts, and these are given by the grace of God to benefit the church or body of Christ. Nineteen gifts are identified in the New Testament. An individual may possess more than one gift; the church as a whole manifests all of the gifts. Believers are responsible to know and exercise their gift(s) as they worship and fellowship with other believers.

Application: As we study God's Word and pray for insight into the gift(s) we have been given, other believers will affirm our gift(s) and God will open up doors of opportunity to exercise them.

Response: Lord Jesus, show me the gift(s) Your Spirit has imparted to me, and direct me in how to use them to build up other believers.

ANGELS

What is man that You are mindful of him, and the son of man that You visit him? For You have made him a little lower than the angels, and You have crowned him with glory and honor.

Psalm 8:4–5

For in the resurrection they neither marry nor are given in marriage, but are like angels of God in heaven.

Matthew 22:30

Nor can they die anymore, for they are equal to the angels and are sons of God, being sons of the resurrection.

Luke 20:36

Are they not all ministering spirits sent forth to minister for those who will inherit salvation?

Hebrews 1:14

Who makes His angels spirits, His ministers a flame of fire.

Psalm 104:4

ANGELS ARE SPIRIT BEINGS created by God. As spirit beings, they do not have physical bodies. In that sense, they are like God who is a personal spirit being. Of course, angels are created, finite beings who are limited in their power and knowledge; whereas God is an infinite being, the Creator of everything that exists, including angels. As spirit beings, angels do not have the limitations of human beings who are part spirit and part body, nor do they have the same needs or capacities. For example, they do not marry or have children, nor do they grow old and die. Angels are more powerful than humans, and in that sense humans are a little lower than the angels. Angels are just like humans however, in being servants of God, messengers who announce His will.

Application: While the holy angels are invisible spirit beings, they are nevertheless real personal beings whom God uses to serve Him and to help us.

Response: Thank you, Lord, for your ministering angels who are present all around us whether we can see them or not.

Now in the sixth month the angel Gabriel was sent by God to a city of Galilee named Nazareth, to a virgin betrothed to a man whose name was Joseph, of the house of David. The virgin's name was Mary.

Luke 1:26–27

To the intent that now the manifold wisdom of God might be made known by the church to the principalities and powers in the heavenly places, according to the eternal purpose which He accomplished in Christ Jesus our Lord.

Ephesians 3:10–11

For in Him dwells all the fullness of the Godhead bodily; and you are complete in Him, who is the head of all principality and power.

Colossians 2:9–10

For by Him all things were created that are in heaven and that are on earth, visible and invisible, whether thrones or dominions or principalities or powers. All things were created through Him and for Him.

Colossians 1:16

BOTH THE HOLY ANGELS and the fallen angels are arranged in order of power and authority. Only one angel, Michael, is called an archangel; he rivals Satan in his power. It was Michael who led the host of holy angels against Satan and his angels, defeating them in a battle in heaven during eternity past. There are other powerful angels in heaven, Gabriel being the only other angel to be named. Other ranks are denoted by titles: principalities, authorities, powers, thrones, might, and dominion. No matter what rank an angel may have, he is subordinate and inferior to his Creator, the One whom the Old Testament identifies as "the Angel of the Lord," that is, the Lord Jesus before He took on human flesh.

Application: Just as there is organization and order among the ranks of angels, so God has ordained specific authority roles to husbands in relation to their wives and to parents in relation to their children.

Response: *I bow my knee to You alone, O Lord, King of the universe and Creator of every creature in heaven and on earth.*

So He drove out the man; and He placed cherubim at the east of the garden of Eden, and a flaming sword which turned every way, to guard the way to the tree of life.

Genesis 3:24

In the year that King Uzziah died, I saw the Lord sitting on a throne, high and lifted up, and the train of His robe filled the temple. Above it stood seraphim; each one had six wings: with two he covered his face, with two he covered his feet, and with two he flew.

Isaiah 6:1–2

And the four living creatures, each having six wings, were full of eyes around and within. And they do not rest day or night saying: "Holy, holy, holy, Lord God Almighty, Who was and is and is to come!"

Revelation 4:8

And behold, an angel of the Lord stood before them, and the glory of the Lord shone around them, and they were greatly afraid.

Luke 2:9

IN ADDITION TO the ranking of angels in order of power and authority, Scripture identifies different types of angels, for example, seraphim and cherubim. The various types of angels correlate closely with the ranking of angels. The names given to the ranks of angels may refer to different types or simply different roles that angels play. They include: archangel, angels, seraphim, cherubim, principalities, authorities, powers, thrones, might, and dominion. The descriptions of these different types of angels vary. Some have four wings, others have six, while still others appear in the form of human beings without wings at all. Whatever their appearance, these angels all have one thing in common: a brightness that reflects the glory of God.

Application: The variety of angels is a reminder that God delights in diversity. As human beings made in His image, we should celebrate the various backgrounds and personalities represented among us.

Response: *O Father, I am awed by the different manifestations of Your glory among the holy angels. May I also reflect Your glory and love to others.*

And Elisha prayed, and said, "Lord, I pray, open his eyes that he may see." Then the Lord opened the eyes of the young man, and he saw. And behold, the mountain was full of horses and chariots of fire all around Elisha.

2 Kings 6:17

Now behold, an angel of the Lord stood by him, and a light shone in the prison; and he struck Peter on the side and raised him up, saying, "Arise quickly!" And his chains fell off his hands.

Acts 12:7

And I saw still another mighty angel coming down from heaven, clothed with a cloud. And a rainbow was on his head, his face was like the sun, and his feet like pillars of fire.

Revelation 10:1

Then I looked, and I heard the voice of many angels around the throne, the living creatures, and the elders; and the number of them was ten thousand times ten thousand, and thousands of thousands.

Revelation 5:11

ALTHOUGH THE ANGELS are spirit beings and invisible by nature, they can become visible to human beings. That is, they may take on bodily form and appear to perform certain functions. Angels have made themselves visible in a selective fashion to some and not to others under the same circumstances. And they have appeared in special visions as well to ordinary sight. In their appearances, they have taken on more than one bodily form: sometimes appearing as ordinary human beings and at other times as unusual winged creatures. They have appeared as warriors with swords, as travelers on a journey, and as glorious, luminous creatures. The purpose of their appearances is to encourage God's people and to strike fear in God's enemies.

Application: Believers have reported unusual occurrences in which those who were about to attack them stopped when they saw many large, shining men with drawn swords. God makes His angels encamp around believers for their protection.

Response: *Whether in my lifetime or in heaven, I look forward to seeing your holy angels with my own eyes, O Lord.*

But the Angel of the LORD called to him from heaven and said, "Abraham, Abraham!" And he said, "Here I am." And He said, "Do not lay your hand on the lad, or do anything to him; for now I know that you fear God, since you have not withheld your son, your only son, from Me."

Genesis 22:11–12

Then as he lay and slept under a broom tree, suddenly an angel touched him, and said to him, "Arise and eat." Then he looked, and there by his head was a cake baked on coals, and a jar of water. So he ate and drank, and lay down again.

1 Kings 19:5–6

Then an angel appeared to Him from heaven, strengthening Him. And being in agony, He prayed more earnestly. And His sweat became like great drops of blood falling down to the ground.

Luke 22:43–44

And while he thought about these things, behold, an angel of the Lord appeared to him in a dream, saying "Joseph, son of David, do not be afraid to take to you Mary your wife, for that which is conceived in her is of the Holy Spirit."

Matthew 1:20

THE HOLY ANGELS play many roles, as recorded in Scripture. The primary role in relation to human beings is as a messenger (the meaning of angel in Greek), a herald proclaiming the will and purpose and judgment of God. Another role is that of protector and deliverer, rescuing God's people from imminent danger. Still another role is that of provider, meeting the needs of believers in many circumstances, both good and evil. One day, angels will take part in the final conflict between God and Satan, with the holy angels defeating the forces of darkness and casting Satan and those who follow him into the lake of fire. Until then, angels will continue watching over God's people and will escort them to heaven if they should die before Jesus returns. In heaven, angels surround the throne of God and proclaim His holiness, prostrating themselves before Him in worship.

Application: We have no idea of how many times angels have been dispatched to our side to meet our needs. But we can all think of some things that have happened for which no other explanation can be given but divine intervention.

Response: It is exciting to realize, O Lord, that your holy angels have been watching over me since I was born!

SATAN AND DEMONS

Again, the devil took Him up on an exceedingly high mountain, and showed Him all the kingdoms of the world and their glory. And he said to Him, "All these things I will give You if You will fall down and worship me."

Matthew 4:8–9

Not a novice, lest being puffed up with pride he fall into the same condemnation as the devil.

1 Timothy 3:6

Do not love the world or the things in the world. If anyone loves the world, the love of the Father is not in him. For all that is in the world—the lust of the flesh, the lust of the eyes, and the pride of life—is not of the Father but is of the world.

1 John 2:15–16

For you have said in your heart: "I will ascend into heaven, I will exalt my throne above the stars of God; I will also sit on the mount of the congregation on the farthest sides of the north; I will ascend above the heights of the clouds, I will be like the Most High."

Isaiah 14:13–14

SATAN (WHICH MEANS *ADVERSARY*) was created as a perfect angel, just as all the other angels were. He was an angel of great intelligence and surpassing beauty. Although created without sin, sin spontaneously erupted in the heart of Satan when he became dissatisfied with his status as a creature and began to desire the place and honor that belongs only to the Creator. In an unbelievable and illogical twist of thinking, Satan began to imagine his throne being placed above God's throne and then set out to make it happen. He infected a large number of other angels with his warped thinking and actually persuaded them to follow him in rebellion against God. This attitude of overestimating himself and allowing his mind to become puffed up is called pride. It was the sin of pride that turned Satan from an innocent and holy angel into a polluted and rebellious angel, who has ever since tried to lead other personal beings into arrogant rebellion against God, and to persuade them to worship Satan instead of God.

Application: Every sin we commit as human beings is rooted in pride and rebellion. What we think and want become more important in our eyes than what God thinks and wants.

Response: Father, I confess that I have a rebel's heart and am all too prone to substitute my will for Yours.

And when He has come, He will convict the world of sin, and of righteousness, and of judgment: . . . of judgment, because the ruler of this world is judged.

John 16:8, 11

And you He made alive who were dead in trespasses and sins, in which you once walked according to the course of this world, according to the prince of the power of the air, the spirit who now works in the sons of disobedience.

Ephesians 2:1–2

For we do not wrestle against flesh and blood, but against principalities, against powers, against the rulers of the darkness of this age, against spiritual hosts of wickedness in the heavenly places.

Ephesians 6:12

We know that we are of God, and the whole world lies under the sway of the wicked one.

1 John 5:19

And He said to them, "I saw Satan fall like lightning from heaven."

Luke 10:18

A LL SIN HAS CONSEQUENCES. Satan's sins of rebelling against God and leading a large number of other angels to follow him in rebellion are no exception. The immediate consequence of their rebellion was that they were cast out of heaven and thrown down to the earth. The fall of Satan and his angels from heaven preceded man's fall. Although Satan could become man's accuser, he could no longer remain in heaven. Heaven is God's dwelling place and no evil can stay there or enter there. Unless sin is repented of, a human being cannot enter heaven. Satan and his angels were confirmed in their sin, unable and unwilling to repent. Their fall from heaven was simply the first stage of God's judgment upon them for their willful rejection of His right to rule over them. Satan became the fallen prince of this world, ruling over the fallen angels and tempting human beings to sin.

Application: All of our sin has consequences. We must never take sin lightly. It causes us to fall out of fellowship with God and may lead others to follow our example.

Response: O God, cause me never to take sin lightly, but to tremble at the thought of offending You. And if I do sin, convict me until I repent and come back into fellowship with You once again.

Watch and pray, lest you enter into temptation. The spirit indeed is willing, but the flesh is weak.

Matthew 26:41

No temptation has overtaken you except such as is common to man; but God is faithful, who will not allow you to be tempted beyond what you are able, but with the temptation will also make the way of escape, that you may be able to bear it.

1 Corinthians 10:13

Let no one say when he is tempted, "I am tempted by God"; for God cannot be tempted by evil, nor does He Himself tempt anyone. But each one is tempted when he is drawn away by his own desires and enticed.

James 1:13–14

Therefore submit to God. Resist the devil and he will flee from you.

James 4:7

ONCE SATAN AND HIS ANGELS, called demons, fell to the earth, they became part of God's plan to rescue the human race. God never tempts anyone, and so Satan willingly played a role God could not play. It was Satan, in the form of a snake, who tempted the first human beings to rebel against God. And Satan and his angels have been tempting human beings ever since, primarily to spite God and to spoil His creation. The avowed enemies of mankind as well as of God, they want to bring as many human beings down to destruction with them as possible. They tempt human beings directly, by appealing to their evil desires, and indirectly, by using the evil world system to appeal to their desires. Either way, they appeal to the fallen, sinful nature of humanity. When Jesus successfully resisted Satan's temptations, He demonstrated perfect obedience to His Father and undid the failure of the first human parents, showing all of us that through the power of God it is possible to resist the Devil.

Application: It is an excuse to say, "The devil made me do it." Satan does tempt us, but we are able to resist him through the power of the Holy Spirit.

Response: O Lord, I do not want to fall for the devil's tricks. Help me to see him coming from a long way off and then to run in the opposite direction.

When evening had come, they brought to Him many who were demon-possessed. And He cast out the spirits with a word, and healed all who were sick.

Matthew 8:16

When He rose early on the first day of the week, He appeared first to Mary Magdalene, out of whom He had cast seven demons.

Mark 16:9

But I say that the things which the Gentiles sacrifice they sacrifice to demons and not to God, and I do not want you to have fellowship with demons.

1 Corinthians 10:20

Now the Spirit expressly says that in latter times some will depart from the faith, giving heed to deceiving spirits and doctrines of demons.

1 Timothy 4:1

You cannot drink the cup of the Lord and the cup of demons; you cannot partake of the Lord's table and of the table of demons.

1 Corinthians 10:21

WHEN SATAN FELL FROM HEAVEN, a large host of angels fell with him. These fallen angels or demons have different ranks and power. They do Satan's bidding and devote themselves to tempting and oppressing all human beings. They may even take up residence in and possess those who do not have a personal relationship with Jesus Christ, but demons cannot possess believers since they are indwelled by the Holy Spirit. Like Satan, the fallen angels can deceive human beings and lead them into sin. For the child of God, the truth of God's Word is the best protection against the lies of Satan and his demons. The Scripture clearly identifies the gods of paganism with demons, and the worship of these gods is demon worship. Paganism is no longer restricted to the past or to primitive peoples. Demon worship and the occult occur more and more openly in Western society. Christians need to be on the alert and actively oppose such demonic activity through the power of the Holy Spirit.

Application: Christians should have nothing to do with seances, Ouija boards, tarot cards, music, or games like Dungeons and Dragons that feature magic and demonic activity. There can be no fellowship between light and darkness.

Response: *Father, forgive me for exposing myself to any influences that could invite demonic activity.*

Yet you shall be brought down to Sheol, to the lowest depths of the Pit.

Isaiah 14:15

Then He will also say to those on the left hand, "Depart from Me, you cursed, into the everlasting fire prepared for the devil and his angels."

Matthew 25:41

And if your foot makes you sin, cut it off. It is better for you to enter life lame, than having two feet, to be cast into hell, into the fire that shall never be quenched.

Mark 9:45

> And the devil, who deceived them, was cast into the lake of fire
> and brimstone where the beast and the false prophet are. And
> they will be tormented day and night forever and ever.
>
> *Revelation 20:10*

CASTING SATAN AND his angels out of heaven to earth was just the first stage in their judgment. One day when Christ returns, Satan will be bound; ultimately he and his followers will be cast into the lake of fire, which is hell. Satan and the demons are not the keepers of hell; they will be among its first occupants. In fact, hell is a place created by God for their eternal punishment and torment. Sad to say, millions upon millions of the human race will suffer the same final fate because they rejected the light and chose darkness instead.

Application: The fate of Satan and his angels should be a sobering reminder of the fate that awaits all who reject Christ and His offer of eternal life. It should motivate Christians everywhere to warn those whose choices are moving them along the road to destruction.

Response: O Father, give me the love and boldness to speak to others about the ultimate consequences of their rejection of Christ, lest they suffer the torments of hell.

MANKIND

This is the book of the genealogy of Adam. In the day that God created man, He made him in the likeness of God. . . And Adam lived one hundred and thirty years, and begot a son in his own likeness, after his image, and named him Seth.

Genesis 5:1, 3

And as we have borne the image of the man of dust, we shall also bear the image of the heavenly Man.

1 Corinthians 15:49

He is the image of the invisible God, the firstborn over all creation.

Colossians 1:15

Then God said, "Let Us make man in Our image, according to Our likeness." . . . So God created man in His own image; in the image of God He created him; male and female He created them.

Genesis 1:26–27

ALTHOUGH LESS POWERFUL and intelligent than the angels, humans stand at the top of the created order in nature because they alone have spirits and are created in the image of God. Because human beings are created in the image of God, they are rational, moral agents who are accountable for their choices, and they have the possibility of a relationship with God.

Alone of all the personal beings in the universe, human beings also have bodies. Since God is a spirit and not a physical being, the creation of mankind in the image of God does not include the body. Nevertheless, humans are whole creatures—spirit, soul, and body—and will not be finally restored to wholeness until the effects of sin on their bodies have also been removed by the resurrection of their bodies when Jesus returns. Because human beings are created in the image of God, each one has intrinsic worth and dignity.

Application: Because all human beings are created in the image of God, they must be respected for that fact and for the fact that Jesus Christ died on the cross for every one of them.

Response: O Lord, help me to look at my fellow man as You do, with compassion and a determination to do good to each one with all my ability.

The Spirit Himself bears witness with our spirit that we are children of God.

Romans 8:16

That you put off, concerning your former conduct, the old man which grows corrupt according to the deceitful lusts, and be renewed in the spirit of your mind.

Ephesians 4:22–23

For the word of God is living and powerful, and sharper than any two-edged sword, piercing even to the division of soul and spirit, and of joints and marrow, and is a discerner of the thoughts and intents of the heart.

Hebrews 4:12

Now may the God of peace Himself sanctify you completely; and may your whole spirit, soul, and body be preserved blameless at the coming of our Lord Jesus Christ.

1 Thessalonians 5:23

ALTHOUGH SOME PEOPLE distinguish only two parts of a human being, body and spirit, which are united to form a living soul, others see three parts: body, mind, and spirit. The mind is the conscious life of a human and includes both rational thoughts and nonrational feelings. This conscious part of man is sometimes called the soul as well as the mind. It is clear from references to the spirit and the soul, the two nonmaterial parts of man, that they are not the same thing. The spirit may be dead while the soul is quite conscious and alive. In the parable Jesus told of the rich man and Lazarus, the rich man in Hades was able to feel pain and rationally dialogue with Abraham across the abyss even though the rich man's spirit was dead.

Salvation affects each part of a human being differently and at different times. When a person becomes a Christian, his dead spirit, the old man or self, is instantly exchanged for a new live spirit, the new man or self. But the new child of God must constantly renew his mind, a lifelong process. Finally, the child of God in heaven will be united to a brand new body when Jesus comes back to this world, bringing the conscious spirits of His own with Him.

Application: The child of God is a human being whose spirit has been made alive, whose mind is in the process of being renewed, and whose body will one day be transformed at Jesus' coming.

Response: Lord Jesus, Your Spirit has assured my new spirit that I am a child of God. One day, I know I shall be just like You in every respect of character.

Behold, I was brought forth in iniquity, and in sin my mother conceived me.

Psalm 51:5

❧❧❧❧

Therefore, just as through one man sin entered the world, and death through sin, and thus death spread to all men, because all sinned. . . .

Romans 5:12

❧❧❧❧

But now, it is no longer I who do it, but sin that dwells in me. For I know that in me (that is, in my flesh) nothing good dwells; for to will is present with me, but how to perform what is good I do not find. For the good that I will to do, I do not do; but the evil I will not to do, that I practice. Now if I do what I will not to do, it is no longer I who do it, but sin that dwells in me.

Romans 7:17–20

❧❧❧❧

For since by man came death, by Man also came the resurrection of the dead. For as in Adam all die, even so in Christ all shall be made alive.

1 Corinthians 15:21–22

❧❧❧❧

So when the woman saw that the tree was good for food, and that it was pleasant to the eyes, and a tree desirable to make one wise, she took of its fruit and ate. She also gave to her husband with her, and he ate.

Genesis 3:6

THE FIRST HUMAN BEINGS on the face of the earth, Adam and Eve, were created in a state of innocence. They had no experiential knowledge of evil. They were placed in a perfect environment and given significant work to do, but they were forbidden to eat of the fruit of the tree in the middle of the garden. They were told it would cost them their lives if they disobeyed. Satan, in the form of a snake, tempted Eve to eat of the fruit. She gave in to Satan's temptation and then offered some of the fruit to Adam. He ate of the fruit also and, along with Eve, fell from a state of innocence. Adam and Eve experienced evil by disobeying God and then felt guilt over breaking God's commandment. Because Adam and Eve fell, the entire human race became infected by an inclination to disobey God. Sin entered the human race and has been transmitted to every generation and to every individual human being ever since. Humans continue to bear the image of God, but an image that has become flawed and corrupted by sin.

Application: Because we are corrupted by sin, we should be profoundly skeptical of our own motives. We are capable of rationalizing and justifying any behavior, even when it directly contradicts an explicit commandment of God.

Response: Father, I confess that I deliberately choose to do wrong even when I know what is right. Please forgive me and cleanse me from all sin.

The next day John saw Jesus coming toward him, and said, "Behold! The Lamb of God who takes away the sin of the world!"

John 1:29

Christ has redeemed us from the curse of the law, having become a curse for us (for it is written, "Cursed is everyone who hangs on a tree").

Galatians 3:13

Not with the blood of goats and calves, but with His own blood He entered the Most Holy Place once for all, having obtained eternal redemption.

Hebrews 9:12

Knowing that you were not redeemed with corruptible things, like silver or gold, from your aimless conduct received by tradition from your fathers, but with the precious blood of Christ, as of a lamb without blemish and without spot.

1 Peter 1:18–19

In Him we have redemption through His blood, the forgiveness of sins, according to the riches of His grace.

Ephesians 1:7

EVEN BEFORE GOD created the world, He planned to create human beings—even though He knew they would choose to disobey Him. And so, at the same time He determined to create humans He also determined to save them from the ultimate consequences of their disobedience. God decided to send His Son to redeem us from the death penalty our sins deserve. Only God's Son was holy enough to become the sin-bearer for all mankind. And only He had the power to confirm our redemption by rising from the dead. Jesus Christ proved Himself to be completely faithful to His Father's commandments. By His obedience to the Father's plan for our redemption from sin's curse, He undid the awful consequences of our rebellion. He redeemed us by His death on the cross, and we are able to receive forgiveness of all our sins and the free gift of eternal life, by placing our faith in His finished work on the cross and His resurrection from death.

Application: Because of our fallen nature, not only are we slaves to sin, but we do not have the means to provide for our liberation from this condition. We are in the position of a bankrupt debtor who is freely forgiven by his creditor; we are spiritually bankrupt and God is our loving, forgiving Creditor.

Response: Lord Jesus, I have nothing in my hand to offer You. All I can do is throw myself on the mercy You so generously offer to me.

And as we have borne the image of the man of dust, we shall also bear the image of the heavenly Man.

1 Corinthians 15:49

Till we all come to the unity of the faith and the knowledge of the Son of God, to a perfect man, to the measure of the stature of the fullness of Christ.

Ephesians 4:13

Who will transform our lowly body that it may be conformed to His glorious body, according to the working by which He is able even to subdue all things to Himself.

Philippians 3:21

And have put on the new man who is renewed in knowledge according to the image of Him who created him.

Colossians 3:10

> For whom He foreknew, He also predestined to be conformed to the image of His Son, that He might be the firstborn among many brethren.
>
> *Romans 8:29*

PART OF GOD'S ETERNAL plan for our redemption was not only that we would be forgiven of all our sins, but that we would become just like His Son, Jesus Christ, in every respect of character. It was not enough that we be declared righteous; God wanted us to be righteous like Jesus Christ. Since sin had spoiled God's image in every part of mankind, every part needed to be restored. Our Spirit is made new and holy at the moment we trust Jesus Christ as our Savior. Our mind must be constantly renewed, with new righteous thoughts, attitudes, and motives substituted for old sinful ones. This is a lifelong process of choosing to obey God's will in the power of the Holy Spirit. As we make these godly choices, our characters are transformed into the likeness of Christ's character. Finally, when Jesus returns to this world, our bodies will be instantly transformed into new resurrection bodies. In the Kingdom of Heaven, we will be just like Jesus Christ in the holiness and wholeness of our body, mind, and spirit.

Application: From God's perspective, the worst thing that can happen to His children is that they remain immature in their spiritual growth.

Response: Heavenly Father, I am Your child, but I do not want to be childish in my faith. I want You to stretch my faith by allowing those circumstances in my life that will force me to live and walk by faith.

SIN

The heart is deceitful above all things, and desperately wicked; who can know it?

Jeremiah 17:9

For from within, out of the heart of men, proceed evil thoughts, adulteries, fornications, murders, thefts, covetousness, wickedness, deceit, licentiousness, an evil eye, blasphemy, pride, foolishness.

Mark 7:21–22

Walk in the Spirit, and you shall not fulfill the lust of the flesh.

Galatians 5:16

Beloved, I beg you as sojourners and pilgrims, abstain from fleshly lusts which war against the soul.

1 Peter 2:11

Let no one say when he is tempted, "I am tempted by God"; for God cannot be tempted by evil, nor does He Himself tempt anyone. But each one is tempted when he is drawn away by his own desires and enticed.

James 1:13–14

THERE ARE THREE MAJOR sources of temptation: the world, the flesh, and the devil. The world and the devil tempt us to sin from the outside, while the flesh tempts us to sin from the inside. Since all temptation appeals to some natural desire, it should not be surprising that the desires themselves should become perverted by sin. The flesh refers to our fallen nature in general and includes all sinful desires and attitudes. Just as there are three major sources of temptation, so there are three kinds of evil desires: the lust of the flesh, the lust of the eyes, and the pride of life. While there is not a one-to-one correlation between the three major sources of temptation and three kinds of evil desires, there is a parallel between the world's temptations and the lust of the eyes, between Satan's temptations and the pride of life, and between the flesh's temptations and the lust of the flesh. In the end, the ultimate source of sin is our own evil heart, that is, our old sin nature that continues to pull at us.

Application: Believers are often watchful for the obvious forms of temptation, but oblivious to the more subtle forms. We need to test the things that appeal to us to see if they increase or dull our obedience to the Lord Jesus Christ.

Response: Holy Spirit, turn the searchlight of the Word of God on my heart and life so I may see any wickedness that might be lurking there and turn away from it.

Speak to all the congregation of the children of Israel, and say to them: "You shall be holy, for I the LORD your God am holy."

Leviticus 19:2

Therefore you shall be perfect, just as your Father in heaven is perfect.

Matthew 5:48

But the Scripture has confined all under sin that the promise by faith in Jesus Christ might be given to those who believe.

Galatians 3:22

But as He who called you is holy, you also be holy in all your conduct.

1 Peter 1:15

For all have sinned and fall short of the glory of God.

Romans 3:23

GOD HAS SET A standard for us to achieve: His own perfect holiness. Anything short of that standard misses the mark and disqualifies us from entering heaven. No matter how moral our behavior may be, we all fall short of God's standard of perfection. It is Christ's holiness that we must incorporate into our lives. It is Christ's glory that the child of God receives and will one day share in heaven. One look at His holiness makes us painfully aware just how far short we really are of God's standard. But one look by faith at the Savior is enough to receive His holiness, which He exchanges for our sin so that we might be qualified to enter heaven.

Application: Apart from a personal relationship with Jesus Christ, even the best of us fall short of what God demands for admission to heaven. That's why we all need a Savior.

Response: *O Lord, I thank You for the day I came to see my spiritual bankruptcy and acknowledged my need of Your grace and mercy. Today I confess my need of personal holiness.*

All we like sheep have gone astray; we have turned, every one, to his own way; and the LORD has laid on Him the iniquity of us all.

Isaiah 53:6

I will give you a new heart and put a new spirit within you; I will take the heart of stone out of your flesh and give you a heart of flesh. I will put My Spirit within you and cause you to walk in My statutes, and you will keep My judgments and do them.

Ezekiel 36:26–27

Therefore, to him who knows to do good and does not do it, to him it is sin.

James 4:17

Whoever commits sin also commits lawlessness, and sin is lawlessness.

1 John 3:4

Knowing this, that our old man was crucified with Him, that the body of sin might be done away with, that we should no longer be slaves of sin.

Romans 6:6

Sin is not only failing to reach God's standard of perfection, it is also breaking God's commandments. As such, it presupposes a knowledge of God's requirements and then a deliberate transgressing of those requirements (as when Adam and Eve disobeyed God's prohibition against eating the fruit of the tree of the knowledge of good and evil). It may involve knowledge of God's special revelation in the Bible, or simply the innate knowledge of the difference between good and evil that conscience provides. Either way, sin is breaking God's moral law (one written on paper, the other inscribed on the heart), and it is always deliberate—an intentional choice to do what is known to be wrong. Because we deliberately and continually break God's moral law, we demonstrate that we are rebels by nature. We not only break God's law, but we are also law-breakers by nature as well as by choice.

Application: Christians should not live defeated lives. By the power of the Spirit, they have the choice on every occasion to obey God.

Response: Lord Jesus, how liberating it is to know I do not have to sin on any occasion! I might choose to, but I do not have to.

I call heaven and earth as witnesses today against you, that I have set before you life and death, blessing and cursing; therefore choose life, that both you and your descendants may live.

Deuteronomy 30:19

Therefore I said to you that you will die in your sins; for if you do not believe that I am He, you will die in your sins.

John 8:24

For if you live according to the flesh you will die; but if by the Spirit you put to death the deeds of the body, you will live.

Romans 8:13

The sting of death is sin, and the strength of sin is the law. But thanks be to God, who gives us the victory through our Lord Jesus Christ.

1 Corinthians 15:56–57

For the wages of sin is death, but the gift of God is eternal life in Christ Jesus our Lord.

Romans 6:23

FROM THE BEGINNING, God told Adam and Eve that breaking His commandments meant they would die. Eve even quoted God's prohibition to Satan when he first approached her. But the devil lied to Eve and told her she would not die if she disobeyed God. Once Adam and Eve sinned, death entered the world. The first part of their being to die was the spirit, and that occurred immediately and completely. Their fellowship with God was broken. The same thing occurs to us whenever we sin. The second part of their being to be affected by sin was their conscious life, their soul. Sin corrupted their thoughts, feelings, attitudes, and motives. That is why Christians constantly have to renew their minds and introduce godly thoughts into their consciousness. The third part of their being to experience death was their physical nature, their body. Our bodies begin to die as soon as we are born and they will all die unless we are alive when Jesus returns. That is why we need brand new bodies, resurrection bodies, just like Jesus' glorified body.

Application: Whenever we break God's commandments, we invite the consequences God said would occur. Whenever we obey God, we put the behavior of our corrupt old natures to death. Sin must die or we will.

Response: Heavenly Father, living for You is the richest, fullest life imaginable! By Your grace, I want to choose life, not death.

But now in Christ Jesus you who once were far off have been made near by the blood of Christ. For He Himself is our peace, who has made both one, and has broken down the middle wall of division between us.

Ephesians 2:13–14

Therefore if there is any consolation in Christ, if any comfort of love, if any fellowship of the Spirit, if any affection and mercy, fulfill my joy by being like-minded, having the same love, being of one accord, of one mind.

Philippians 2:1–2

If we say that we have fellowship with Him, and walk in darkness, we lie and do not practice the truth. But if we walk in the light as He is in the light, we have fellowship with one another, and the blood of Jesus Christ His Son cleanses us from all sin.

1 John 1:6–7

That which we have seen and heard we declare to you, that you also may have fellowship with us; and truly our fellowship is with the Father and with His Son Jesus Christ.

1 John 1:3

G OD CREATED HUMAN BEINGS to have close, intimate fellowship with Him. When Adam and Eve rebelled against God, their spirits died and they experienced a conscious alienation from God. In their guilt, they tried to hide themselves from Him. And so it is with us when we sin. For unbelievers, fellowship with God is permanently broken until they repent and are reconciled to God. For believers, fellowship with God is temporarily broken by sin but is restored when sin is confessed and forsaken. Fellowship means commonness or sharing something in common. Believers have fellowship with one another and with God because they share the presence of the Holy Spirit in common. Because of His presence, we can address God as Father and one another as brother or sister. We are all part of one family, God's family.

Application: If God has reconciled us to Himself, how can we do otherwise than to be reconciled to one another? It is sin and selfishness that separate us from one another and from God.

Response: O Father, I was once a stranger and You took me in. Help me to reach out to the friendless and befriend them. May they experience the love of Christ and the fellowship of the Holy Spirit through me.

SALVATION

Now when the Gentiles heard this, they were glad and glorified the word of the Lord. And as many as had been appointed to eternal life believed.

Acts 13:48

For whom He foreknew, He also predestined to be conformed to the image of His Son, that He might be the first-born among many brethren.

Romans 8:29

For He says to Moses, "I will have mercy on whomever I will have mercy, and I will have compassion on whomever I will have compassion." So then it is not of him who wills, nor of him who runs, but of God who shows mercy.

Romans 9:15–16

Just as He chose us in Him before the foundation of the world, that we should be holy and without blame before Him in love, having predestined us to adoption as sons by Jesus Christ to Himself, according to the good pleasure of His will.

Ephesians 1:4–5

GOD MUST CHOOSE MANKIND because fallen sinful people refuse to choose God. God's choice or election of some of His rebellious creatures to become His children is entirely an act of undeserved kindness. He could have let us all pay the penalty our sins deserve, but instead He fixed His love on some of us and granted us the free gift of eternal life. We were all spiritually dead to begin with, unwilling and unable to believe in Jesus Christ as Savior and Lord. God had to intervene and enable us to exercise saving faith in His Son. His choice of us is always now to God, and so is our response of faith. He elects, and we believe. He makes us alive spiritually and at the same time grants us the gift of faith so we can believe. The wonder is not that He does not save everyone, but that He saves anyone. He is sovereign and out of love chooses to save some.

Application: As proud human beings, we are tempted to resent the fact that our salvation is all of God's doing and none of ours. But how grateful we should be that our eternal life does not depend on our whim or caprice. The same God who took the initiative to save us is the One who keeps us securely in His fold.

Response: O Lord, I do not know why You should choose me, undeserving as I am. But I am so thankful that You did!

No one can come to Me unless the Father who sent Me draws him; and I will raise him up at the last day.

John 6:44

And that He might make known the riches of His glory on the vessels of mercy, which He had prepared beforehand for glory, even us whom He called, not of the Jews only, but also of the Gentiles.

Romans 9:23–24

God is faithful, by whom you were called into the fellowship of His Son, Jesus Christ our Lord.

1 Corinthians 1:9

Who has saved us and called us with a holy calling, not according to our works, but according to His own purpose and grace which was given to us in Christ Jesus before time began.

2 Timothy 1:9

> And we know that all things work together for good to those who
> love God, to those who are the called according to His purpose.
>
> *Romans 8:28*

WHILE GOD IS OUTSIDE of time and does not change, we are finite creatures with a past, present, and future, and we do change. Whereas God's election of us to be His own was fixed in eternity past, His calling of us takes place at a specific point in time. In addition to the general call given through the preaching of the gospel, there is a day in our lives as believers when God calls our name, and when He does we answer. Spiritually speaking, we are all in the position of Jesus' earthly friend, Lazarus. We begin our spiritual journey by being dead, and then Jesus calls our name and we come alive. Jesus calls us by creating a spiritual hunger within our hearts and convicting us of our sin and our need of a Savior. We are like the prodigal son in Jesus' parable who "comes to himself" in a far country. We have a compelling desire to return to the Father and confess our sins. When we respond to the Father's call, we find Him reaching out to draw us to Himself in love. We were lost, and now we are found. We were dead, and now we are alive.

Application: Whether we remember the date or not, there is a day when each one of us hears our heavenly Father calling us out of darkness and into light. That is the day when our spiritual eyes are opened and we see Jesus as He really is and ourselves as we really are.

Response: Lord Jesus, I remember vividly the day when my heart burned within me and my hunger for Your love and forgiveness drew me to You.

And he believed in the LORD, and He accounted it to him for righteousness.

Genesis 15:6

To demonstrate at the present time His righteousness, that He might be just and the justifier of the one who has faith in Jesus.

Romans 3:26

For I am not ashamed of the gospel of Christ, for it is the power of God to salvation for everyone who believes, for the Jew first and also for the Greek. For in it the righteousness of God is revealed from faith to faith; as it is written, "The just shall live by faith."

Romans 1:16–17

For He made Him who knew no sin to be sin for us, that we
might become the righteousness of God in Him.

2 Corinthians 5:21

NOT ONLY DOES GOD set His love upon us from all of eternity and call
us into a personal relationship with Him at a given point in time,
but the moment we respond by faith to His call He declares us righteous,
or just, enough to enter heaven. That declaration is called justification
and is a legal term that signifies vindication by the One who is the Judge
of the universe. God is perfectly righteous and holy in His person and in
His law. As sinners, we are unrighteous and unholy in our person and
lawbreakers in our behavior. There is no way we can enter a holy heaven
apart from some payment for all our sins. And there is no way that a holy
God can pardon us without at the same time carrying out the just sen-
tence of death He pronounced on sin before any sin was ever committed. By sending His perfect Son into the world to pay the penalty our sin
deserves, God could be merciful to us while remaining completely just.
Jesus Christ became the payment for our sin, and we were declared just
by a holy God when we repented of our sin and placed our faith in His
death on the cross. Christ's righteousness was credited to us in exchange
for our sin. On that basis, we can enter heaven.

Application: The difference between human and divine pardon is that
in divine pardon someone else pays for our wrongdoing. Human
pardons may be quite arbitrary, but God's pardon is just.

Response: *O Lord, I know what a sinner I am, yet the moment I repented
and trusted Jesus as my Savior and Lord, You looked at me as if I had
never sinned!*

Create in me a clean heart, O God, and renew a steadfast spirit within me.

Psalm 51:10

Sanctify them by Your truth. Your word is truth.

John 17:17

I beseech you therefore, brethren, by the mercies of God, that you present your bodies a living sacrifice, holy, acceptable to God, which is your reasonable service. And do not be conformed to this world, but be transformed by the renewing of your mind, that you may prove what is that good and acceptable and perfect will of God.

Romans 12:1–2

For by one offering He has perfected forever those who are being sanctified.

Hebrews 10:14

For this is the will of God, your sanctification: . . .

1 Thessalonians 4:3a

GOD EXPECTS MORE from those He has eternally loved, called, and justified than that they become qualified to enter heaven. He has a wonderful plan for our lives, both now and in eternity: He wants us to become just like His Son, Jesus Christ. Jesus is holy, and we need to become holy. Whereas our justification is entirely an act of God, our sanctification—our being made holy—is a cooperative venture. It involves our willing obedience to Christ as Lord in every area of our lives. To the extent that we obey Him, we become like Him and demonstrate our love for Him. The chief impediment in the sanctification process is our sin, the residue of our old sin nature that is still with us. We want to obey Christ, but we sometimes choose to follow our old sinful impulses. Nevertheless, for a child of God, it is always possible to obey Christ. He has given us His Holy Spirit to dwell within us to enable us to obey Him, but we must cooperate with Him.

Application: We live in an age that does not value holy living. We must resolve to obey God and resist the pull of the world by the power of the Holy Spirit.

Response: Father, I confess that I am too influenced by the world. I ask you to cleanse me from all unrighteousness and to fill my heart with a burning desire for personal holiness.

You will guide me with Your counsel, and afterward receive me to glory.

Psalm 73:24

Father, I desire that they also whom You gave Me may be with Me where I am, that they may behold My glory which You have given Me; for You loved Me before the foundation of the world.

John 17:24

To them God willed to make known what are the riches of the glory of this mystery among the Gentiles: which is Christ in you, the hope of glory.

Colossians 1:27

For it was fitting for Him, for whom are all things and by whom are all things, in bringing many sons to glory, to make the author of their salvation perfect through sufferings.

Hebrews 2:10

Moreover, whom He predestined, these He also called; whom He called, these He also justified; and whom He justified, these He also glorified.

Romans 8:30

THE GOAL OF SALVATION for believers is to share heaven with the Lord Jesus Christ. Heaven is also called glory, and when believers are ushered into heaven, they are glorified. The sanctification process is completed when a Christian enters heaven because the last vestige of sin has been removed. It is not only that believers will be like Jesus Christ in every respect of character, they will also have a resurrected body just like His. When Jesus returns, a glorified spirit will be joined to a glorified body, one free from the corruption of sin and fit for heaven. Jesus is not only in glory, He is the Lord of glory. We will worship and serve Him for all eternity, sharing in His glory. Not only is heaven glory, but it is the place where the radiance of Christ's glory will be the only illumination required.

Application: God gives us assurance that He will complete our salvation, including giving us brand new bodies like Christ's body. We can be as sure of heaven as if we were already there.

Response: O Lord Jesus, how I long to see You face to face, whether You return while I am still alive or I go home to be with You in heaven first!

DISCIPLESHIP

Oh, continue Your lovingkindness to those who know You, and Your righteousness to the upright in heart.

Psalm 36:10

I am the good shepherd; and I know My sheep, and am known by My own.

John 10:14

But now after you have known God, or rather are known by God, how is it that you turn again to the weak and beggarly elements, to which you desire again to be in bondage?

Galatians 4:9

But indeed I also count all things loss for the excellence of the knowledge of Christ Jesus my Lord, for whom I have suffered the loss of all things, and count them as rubbish, that I may gain Christ . . . that I may know Him and the power of His resurrection, and the fellowship of His sufferings, being conformed to His death.

Philippians 3:8, 10

And this is eternal life, that they may know You, the only true God, and Jesus Christ whom You have sent.

John 17:3

DISCIPLESHIP, LEARNING FROM and following Christ, begins with knowing Him. To know Christ is not to know about Him, but to know Him by personal acquaintance. We get to know Him through hearing and reading the Word of God. The Holy Spirit is the One who makes the Bible come alive so that Jesus, as it were, steps out of the pages of Scripture and greets us, extending His hand for us to grasp by faith. Jesus is a person whom we can know personally, and with whom we can have an intimate, personal relationship. As important as knowing Christ is, it is equally important that He know us. When Christ returns He will call us by name and give us new resurrection bodies just like His. To those who do not know Christ, He will say, "I never knew you. Depart from me." It is eternally important that we know Christ and that He knows us. Once we know Him, we can be His disciples.

Application: A person can have a great deal of knowledge about God and still be lost if that individual does not have a personal relationship with Jesus Christ. By contrast, even a little child who knows very little about God can be saved by simply trusting Jesus Christ as Savior and Lord.

Response: *Lord Jesus, I will never forget the day I met You and invited You to come into my heart. How glad I am that You live within me!*

Take My yoke upon you and learn from Me, for I am gentle and lowly in heart, and you will find rest for your souls.

Matthew 11:29

And you shall know the truth, and the truth shall make you free.

John 8:32

But you have not so learned Christ, if indeed you have heard Him and have been taught by Him, as the truth is in Jesus.

Ephesians 4:20–21

For I have given to them the words which You have given Me; and they have received them, and have known surely that I came forth from You; and they have believed that You sent Me.

John 17:8

WE CANNOT FOLLOW Christ unless we know where He wants to lead us, that is, what truths He wants us to incorporate into our lives. Learning from Christ is accomplished through Bible study and meditation on God's Word. It is also achieved through the lessons God teaches us through life's experiences, but in a special sense, learning from Christ consists in learning the truths He taught during His earthly ministry. This is accomplished through a careful study of the New Testament, by noting specifically the principles Christ taught. Learning from Christ also consists in observing what He did in various situations, how He responded to different kinds of people, and how He tried to please His Father. Jesus is the Master, the greatest Teacher who ever lived. He told us to search the Scriptures and learn of Him.

Application: Every word that Jesus taught came from God the Father. If we believe human teachers, should we not believe the Son of God? We may stake our eternal life on the words He taught.

Response: *Lord Jesus, I do not just believe Your words, I believe You. You are the very embodiment of truth, and You have set me free.*

Then Jesus said to His disciples, "If anyone desires to come after Me, let him deny himself, and take up his cross, and follow Me."

Matthew 16:24

∽∽∽∽

A disciple is not above his teacher, but everyone who is perfectly trained will be like his teacher.

Luke 6:40

∽∽∽∽

If I then, your Lord and Teacher, have washed your feet, you also ought to wash one another's feet. For I have given you an example, that you should do as I have done to you.

John 13:14–15

∽∽∽∽

Imitate me, just as I also imitate Christ.

1 Corinthians 11:1

For to this you were called, because Christ also suffered for us,
leaving us an example, that you should follow His steps.

1 Peter 2:21

THE SECOND PART of discipleship is to follow Christ, that is to imitate Him and become like Him. He wants us to follow His example and do what He has taught us to do. There is a price to be paid for following Jesus; we must crucify our selfish desires and refrain from anything that would displease Him. We must identify so strongly with Christ that we are willing to share in His suffering as well as in His victory over sin and death, to feel His compassion for the lost and His anger at hypocrisy and injustice. As followers of Christ we share His fellowship with the Father and His empowerment by the Holy Spirit. We strive to advance His kingdom and lift up His name. We make His priorities our priorities.

Application: As believers, we should follow Christ so closely that others can follow our example.

Response: Lord Jesus, I want others to see You living in me even as I follow in Your footsteps. More than anything, I want to be like You!

Not everyone who says to Me, "Lord, Lord," shall enter the kingdom of heaven, but he who does the will of My Father in heaven.

Matthew 7:21

But why do you call Me "Lord, Lord," and do not do the things which I say?

Luke 6:46

A new commandment I give to you, that you love one another; as I have loved you, that you also love one another. By this all will know that you are My disciples, if you have love for one another.

John 13:34–35

For this is the love of God, that we keep His commandments. And His commandments are not burdensome.

1 John 5:3

If you love Me, keep My commandments.

John 14:15

WE CANNOT FOLLOW Christ unless we obey Him. The true test of our discipleship is whether we do what Christ says. Jesus is not only our Teacher and our example; He is also our Lord. We must not only be hearers of Christ's Word, but doers as well. We obey Christ because we love Him and desire to please Him. In obeying Christ, we are also following His example for He emphasized over and over again that He had come to do the Father's will. Nothing substitutes for obedience, not even religious activity. If the Christian life is reduced to its essence, it is making one choice after another out of love and obedience to Christ. To obey Christ is to demonstrate our love to Him, thus showing the world that we belong to Him. By contrast, all sin is deliberate disobedience to God's commandments.

Application: We cannot love Jesus in our hearts if we do not love Jesus with our lives.

Response: *I have learned there is no other way to be happy in You, Lord, but to trust and obey.*

And He said to them, "Go into all the world and preach the gospel to every creature."

Mark 16:15

❦

But you shall receive power when the Holy Spirit has come upon you; and you shall be witnesses to Me in Jerusalem, and in all Judea and Samaria, and to the end of the earth.

Acts 1:8

❦

For the love of Christ constrains us, because we judge thus: that if One died for all, then all died; . . . Therefore we are ambassadors for Christ, as though God were pleading through us: we implore you on Christ's behalf, be reconciled to God.

2 Corinthians 5:14, 20

> Go therefore and make disciples of all the nations, baptizing
> them in the name of the Father and of the Son and of the Holy
> Spirit, teaching them to observe all things that I have commanded
> you. . . .

Matthew 28:19–20

IF WE ARE LEARNING from Christ, following in His footsteps, and obeying His commandments, we cannot help wanting to tell the world who He is and what He has done for us. Jesus' last commandment, the Great Commission, instructs us to make disciples of every nation. To do this, we must first witness to people about Jesus Christ and tell them how they can come to know Him. Witnessing for Christ begins with evangelism, sharing the Good News of His death, burial, and resurrection and explaining how salvation comes by believing in Him and His sacrifice on the cross. Witnessing for Christ also involves encouraging those who have trusted Him to become His disciples.

Application: Someone was faithful and told us about salvation through Christ; we must show the same love to others so they will have an opportunity to trust Him.

Response: Lord Jesus, how can I possibly keep such Good News to myself? You have filled my heart with Your love and I want to tell others about it.

STEWARDSHIP

Then the LORD God took the man and put him in the garden of Eden to tend and keep it.

Genesis 2:15

Six years you shall sow your field, and six years you shall prune your vineyard, and gather in its fruit; but in the seventh year there shall be a sabbath of solemn rest for the land, a sabbath to the LORD. You shall neither sow your field nor prune your vineyard.

Leviticus 25:3–4

What is man that You are mindful of him, and the son of man that You visit him? . . . You have made him to have dominion over the works of Your hands; You have put all things under his feet.

Psalm 8:4, 6

> Then God said, "Let Us make man in Our image, according to Our likeness; let them have dominion over the fish of the sea, over the birds of the air, and over the cattle, over all the earth and over every creeping thing that creeps on the earth."
>
> *Genesis 1:26*

WHEN GOD CREATED human beings in His own image He gave them an exalted position in the created order. They were not only superior to all other earthly creatures but were given the right to rule those creatures. In addition, they were given a responsibility to care for the earth and all its creatures. Adam was given the right to name the other creatures and was charged with taking care of the garden. Later, when God gave the Law to His people, He included specific instructions for caring for the earth so its nutrients could be replenished. God gave human beings the authority to rule and tame the natural order, and the responsibility to care for this world in His name. When they fail to do so, He holds them accountable. One day, when humanity's redemption is complete, the created order will also be transformed into a new heaven and a new earth.

Application: This is our Father's world, and we dare not treat His world as if it were a disposable, throwaway product. When we act as faithful stewards of God's world, we please Him and bring glory to His name.

Response: Heavenly Father, You made the world and called it good. May I be a faithful steward and care for Your world and all Your creatures.

For if I preach the gospel, I have nothing to boast of, for necessity is laid upon me; yes, woe is me if I do not preach the gospel! For if I do this willingly, I have a reward; but if against my will, I have been entrusted with a stewardship.

1 Corinthians 9:16–17

To me, who am less than the least of all the saints, this grace was given, that I should preach among the Gentiles the unsearchable riches of Christ.

Ephesians 3:8

As each one has received a gift, minister it to one another, as good stewards of the manifold grace of God.

1 Peter 4:10

Let a man so consider us as servants of Christ and stewards of the mysteries of God. Moreover it is required in stewards that one be found faithful.

1 Corinthians 4:1–2

BELIEVERS HAVE BEEN MADE stewards of God's message of salvation to the world. God did not entrust this message to angels but to us. That stewardship was given as part of Christ's final commandment to His disciples. His charge to carry the gospel to the whole world is called the Great Commission. Originally, God had given the nation of Israel the assignment to be a light to the other nations of the world. But when the people of Israel proved to be untrustworthy with that message, God transferred the responsibility for proclaiming the gospel to the church. When Christ returns to this world for His own, He will examine our lives to see if we have been faithful in carrying out our responsibility to warn those who are perishing in their sin to repent and come to Christ.

Application: When we go to a bank or trust company to invest our money, we are placing our treasure into the hands of an organization that was designed for that purpose. When God places the gospel message in the hands of His church, He is doing the same thing.

Response: *O Lord, You have entrusted me with the Word of Life. May I be found faithful in sharing it with those who are perishing.*

LORD, make me to know my end, and what is the measure of my days, that I may know how frail I am.

Psalm 39:4

So teach us to number our days, that we may gain a heart of wisdom.

Psalm 90:12

To everything there is a season, a time for every purpose under heaven.

Ecclesiastes 3:1

Come now, you who say, "Today or tomorrow we will go to such and such a city, spend a year there, buy and sell, and make a profit"; whereas you do not know what will happen tomorrow. For what is your life? It is even a vapor that appears for a little time and then vanishes away. Instead you ought to say, "If the Lord wills, we shall live and do this or that."

James 4:13–15

See then that you walk circumspectly, not as fools but as wise, redeeming the time, because the days are evil. Therefore do not be unwise, but understand what the will of the Lord is.

Ephesians 5:15–17

As BELIEVERS, WE are to be stewards of the gifts God has put in our hands, beginning with the time He has allotted us. From the perspective of eternity, our time upon the earth is like a quickly drawn breath. Life is short and not to be wasted. On the contrary, we are to redeem the time, to make full use of the days, hours, and seconds God gives us. God has a wonderful plan for our lives that is revealed one day at a time. Each day has enough hours to do all that our Father expects us to do, and He will show us His will through the circumstances of our lives. He only expects us to put Him first and to be obedient to His revealed will. Jesus showed us how to put God first by spending long seasons in prayer. If Jesus needed fellowship with the Father to accomplish the divine purpose, so do we. And if Jesus yielded Himself each day to do the Father's will, so must we. That is being a good steward of time.

Application: While our lives are relatively brief, they can be full of significance if we dedicate them to worshiping God and doing His will.

***Response:** O Lord, may Your will be done in my life this day. You have given me this day as a gift, and I want to use it to bring honor to You.*

Having then gifts differing according to the grace that is given to us, let us use them: if prophecy, let us prophesy in proportion to our faith; or ministry, let us use it in our ministering; he who teaches, in teaching.

Romans 12:6–7

But one and the same Spirit works all these things, distributing to each one individually as He wills.

1 Corinthians 12:11

Till I come, give attention to reading, to exhortation, to doctrine. Do not neglect the gift that is in you, which was given to you by prophecy with the laying on of the hands of the presbytery.

1 Timothy 4:13–14

Therefore I remind you to stir up the gift of God which is in you through the laying on of my hands.

2 Timothy 1:6

Now there are diversities of gifts, but the same Spirit . . . But the manifestation of the Spirit is given to each one for the profit of all.

1 Corinthians 12:4, 7

NOT ONLY MUST we be good stewards of our time, but we must also be good stewards of the talents and gifts God has given us. Our talents are the natural abilities He created in us at birth, and our gifts are spiritual abilities we received at the time we became Christians. We must use our God-given talents to benefit mankind in general, and we must use our Spirit-given gifts to build up fellow believers in the body of Christ. Both our talents and our gifts may be cultivated or neglected. We must use them or lose them. They are not to be squandered on ourselves or flaunted with boastful pride. We may have many or few talents or gifts, but whatever the number, they are to be faithfully used for the glory of God and the good of others. Just as God has a purpose in the amount of time He grants to us, so He has a purpose in talents and gifts He has given us. We will be held accountable at the judgment seat of Christ for our use of both.

Application: Sadly, Christians often spend more time trying to determine what spiritual gifts they have than using them to benefit others. Spiritual gifts are like carpenter's tools: If we don't use them, they tend to become rusty.

Response: Lord Jesus, forgive me for neglecting the spiritual gifts You have given me. Help me to faithfully use the gifts I received when I was saved.

"Bring all the tithes into the storehouse, that there may be food in My house, and prove Me now in this," says the LORD of hosts, "If I will not open for you the windows of heaven and pour out for you such blessing that there will not be room enough to receive it."

Malachi 3:10

Give, and it will be given to you: good measure, pressed down, shaken together, and running over will be put into your bosom. For with the same measure that you use, it will be measured back to you.

Luke 6:38

I have shown you in every way, by laboring like this, that you must support the weak. And remember the words of the Lord Jesus, that He said, "It is more blessed to give than to receive."

Acts 20:35

So let each one give as he purposes in his heart, not grudgingly or of necessity; for God loves a cheerful giver.

2 Corinthians 9:7

As with our time and talent, we are to be stewards of our treasure, the material resources God places in our hands. There are important principles relating to the stewardship of material resources taught in the Bible. To begin with, everything belongs to God by virtue of creation and we are simply returning to God what is His already. Secondly, we give to God voluntarily, in accordance with His blessing, and not legalistically, because we have to. He chooses to use us as channels to bless others and to meet their needs. In God's economy, it is more blessed to give than to receive. Finally, we cannot outgive God. He will always return a blessing more abundant than anything we give.

Application: A young Christian once asked an elderly believer with a meager income, "How can you afford to tithe?" To which the older man replied, "I cannot afford not to tithe!" He had learned the valuable lesson that God is no man's debtor.

Response: *Heavenly Father, what a joy it is to return a portion of what You have first given me! It all belongs to You anyway.*

RELATIONSHIPS

So then, they are no longer two but one flesh. Therefore what God has joined together, let not man separate.

Matthew 19:6

Let the husband render to his wife the affection due her, and likewise also the wife to her husband. The wife does not have authority over her own body, but the husband does. And likewise the husband does not have authority over his own body but the wife does.

1 Corinthians 7:3–4

Likewise you wives, be submissive to your own husbands, that even if some do not obey the word, they, without a word, may be won by the conduct of their wives. . . . Likewise you husbands, dwell with them with understanding, giving honor to the wife, as to the weaker vessel, and as being heirs together of the grace of life, that your prayers may not be hindered.

1 Peter 3:1, 7

Wives, submit to your own husbands, as to the Lord . . .
Husbands, love your wives, just as Christ also loved the church
and gave Himself for it.

Ephesians 5:22, 25

MARRIAGE WAS GOD'S idea—He created human beings in His own image as both male and female. He brought the first woman to the first man and commanded them to be fruitful and multiply. But when Adam and Eve sinned, the institution of marriage was corrupted by the fall. God reestablished order in the family, giving the husband a leadership role and the wife a nurturing and supportive role. Both husband and wife are equal in their spiritual standing before God. Each is to submit to the other, putting the needs of the other ahead of personal needs. God's intent from the beginning was for a permanent union between husband and wife, and for a relationship that would take priority over all other human relationships. Husbands are to love their wives and sacrifice for them just as Christ loved the church and sacrificed Himself for her. Wives are to honor their husbands just as all believers are to honor their Lord. By carrying out these God-given roles, husbands and wives are not only fulfilled but they demonstrate to the world the relationship of Christ to His church.

Application: If every husband and every wife saw their spouse as God's greatest gift in life, they would enjoy all the blessings God had in mind when He created them for one another.

Response: Father, thank you that we all stand equal before you. Help us to love and serve each other as you loved and served the church.

Honor your father and your mother, as the LORD your God has commanded you, that your days may be long, and that it may be well with you in the land which the LORD your God is giving you.

Deuteronomy 5:16

And these words which I command you today shall be in your heart; you shall teach them diligently to your children, and shall talk of them when you sit in your house, when you walk by the way, when you lie down, and when you rise up.

Deuteronomy 6:6–7

Children, obey your parents in all things, for this is well pleasing to the Lord. Fathers, do not provoke your children, lest they become discouraged.

Colossians 3:20–21

Train up a child in the way he should go, and when he is old he will not depart from it.

Proverbs 22:6

GOD ORDAINED MARRIAGE, in part, for the procreation of the human race. Since all of the descendants of Adam and Eve were born after the fall, every child has entered the world with a sin nature that inclines toward sinning. This is why parents must endeavor to lead their children to a saving knowledge of Jesus Christ at the earliest age possible. Parents need to teach their children the truths of the Bible at every opportunity, giving them the resources they need to grow into mature, godly young men and women. Parents must also set an example of godly living before their children to reinforce what they have taught and to give their children godly patterns to imitate. For their part, children need to learn to respect and obey their parents. They must be taught that the length and quality of their lives is related to how they treat their parents.

Application: There is no more worthy task in the world than bringing up children who honor God. The church must make the training of godly parents its number one priority.

Response: Heavenly Father, You have taught us the patterns for developing healthy relationships in our families. Help us to be faithful to your example.

You shall not defraud your neighbor, nor rob him. The wages of him who is hired shall not remain with you all night until morning.

Leviticus 19:13

There is nothing better for a man than that he should eat and drink, and that his soul should enjoy good in his labor. This also, I saw, was from the hand of God.

Ecclesiastes 2:24

And whatever you do, do it heartily, as to the Lord and not to men, knowing that from the Lord you will receive the reward of the inheritance; for you serve the Lord Christ.

Colossians 3:23–24

Masters, give your servants what is just and fair, knowing that you also have a Master in heaven.

Colossians 4:1

Servants, be obedient to those who are your masters according to the flesh, with fear and trembling, in sincerity of heart, as to Christ; not with eyeservice, as men-pleasers, but as servants of Christ, doing the will of God from the heart.

Ephesians 6:5–6

WORK IS A calling of God. Some of us work for others and some of us work for ourselves. Even those who work for themselves have some sort of relationship to those who buy their products or use their services. The Bible teaches employees to be satisfied with their wages and employers to be fair and just to their employees, not treating them harshly or withholding their wages. Employees are to respect their employers and do their work heartily, as if they were working for the Lord Himself. Employees should perform their duties faithfully, even when their employer is not looking, and they should be men and women of integrity, examples to others in the workplace. Both Christian employees and employers should remember that they have a Master in heaven Who will inspect the performance of their duties some day.

Application: How do our work habits reflect on our Christian testimony? Do they speak well of Christ and His church? Is Christ pleased with what He sees?

Response: Lord Jesus, one day I shall stand before you to give an account of the work I did throughout my life. I want more than anything to hear you say, "Well done" on that day.

You are the light of the world. A city that is set on a hill cannot be hidden. . . . Let your light so shine before men, that they may see your good works and glorify your Father in heaven.

Matthew 5:14, 16

Therefore I exhort first of all that supplications, prayers, intercessions, and giving of thanks be made for all men, for kings and all who are in authority, that we may lead a quiet and peaceable life in all godliness and reverence.

1 Timothy 2:1–2

Therefore submit yourselves to every ordinance of man for the Lord's sake, whether to the king as supreme, or to governors, as to those who are sent by him for the punishment of evildoers and for the praise of those who do good.

1 Peter 2:13–14

Then Jesus answered and said to them "Render to Caesar the things that are Caesar's, and to God the things that are God's."

Mark 12:17

CHRISTIANS ARE CITIZENS of heaven first and of political entities on earth second. Whatever the political structure may be, believers have specific duties to discharge on behalf of their government and its leaders if they are to be obedient to God. Both in Old and New Testament times, believers have lived in secular societies that were openly hostile to their faith. In all of those contexts, people of faith were to pray for the good of the sovereign, to obey the laws of the land, and to conduct themselves in such a way that the political powers involved would have no legitimate cause to accuse them or punish them. They were to pay their taxes, perform their civic responsibilities, and render appropriate honor to the sovereign. In it all, they were to give their primary allegiance to God and their secondary allegiance to the state. Believers have a moral and spiritual responsibility to promote righteousness and oppose evil through every legitimate means and to petition their government to do the same.

Application: Believers in the Lord Jesus Christ are salt and light in the world. We must not withhold our godly influence upon society. God expects, indeed commands, us as Christian citizens to let our light shine.

***Response:** Father, forgive me for my failure to be active in Your name. I cannot complain about the evil in my society if I do nothing to stop it.*

And it was so, when he had finished speaking to Saul, that the soul of Jonathan was knit to the soul of David, and Jonathan loved him as his own soul. . . . And Jonathan took off the robe that was on him and gave it to David, with his armor, even to his sword and his bow and his belt.

1 Samuel 18:1, 4

As iron sharpens iron, so a man sharpens the countenance of his friend.

Proverbs 27:17

Greater love has no one than this, than to lay down one's life for his friends. You are My friends if you do whatever I command you. No longer do I call you servants, for a servant does not know what his master is doing; but I have called you friends, for all things that I heard from My Father I have made known to you.

John 15:13–15

A man who has friends must himself be friendly, but there is a friend who sticks closer than a brother.

Proverbs 18:24

ONE RELATIONSHIP THAT parallels all other human relationships is that of friends. Husbands and wives may be friends; parents and children may be friends; employers and employees may be friends; and even politicians and their constituents may be friends. Finally, and most pervasively, two individuals may be friends who have no other relationship to one another. The Bible teaches certain principles about friendship. If we want to have friends, we must be a friend. That means caring for, showing an interest in, and spending time with others. It means sharing thoughts and innermost feelings with them. Friendship is a reciprocal relationship. True friends always seek what is in the other person's best interest.

Application: As Christians, we should demonstrate to our friends all the dimensions of friendship taught in the Word of God, giving to others as well as receiving from others.

Response: *O Lord, I have been far too selfish and demanding of my friends. May I begin to show them the sacrificial kind of friendship You have shown me.*

THE CHURCH

I do not pray for these alone, but also for those who will believe in Me through their word; that they all may be one, as You, Father, are in Me, and I in You; that they also may be one in Us, that the world may believe that You sent Me.

John 17:20–21

For as we have many members in one body, but all the members do not have the same function, so we, being many, are one body in Christ, and individually members of one another.

Romans 12:4–5

For you are all sons of God through faith in Christ Jesus. . . . There is neither Jew nor Greek, there is neither slave nor free, there is neither male nor female; for you are all one in Christ Jesus.

Galatians 3:26, 28

For as the body is one and has many members, but all the members of that one body, being many, are one body, so also is Christ. . . . Now you are the body of Christ, and members individually.

1 Corinthians 12:12, 27

ALL THOSE WHO believe in Christ form an invisible body called the church. Because God is their heavenly Father, they are all brothers and sisters. They have been born again as children of God and belong to the family of God. As such, all Christians are related to and affected by one another. If one is blessed, all are blessed. If one suffers, all suffer. If one sins, the testimony of the whole body is damaged. Believers are mutually dependent on one another for their spiritual health and growth. No Christian is an island but is connected to every other believer by a common faith in a common Lord. God has formed His church out of every tribe, tongue, and people, erasing all national, ethnic, racial, social, and gender distinctions. We are all equal as members of the body of Christ, although we play complementary roles within that body. No role and no member of the body is insignificant or unimportant. We are to care for one another, build up one another, and bear with one another.

Application: As members of the body of Christ we need and depend on each other, and that is the way God designed it.

Response: O Lord, help me to be a worthy member of your church, reaching out to those in need and living as an example of your love and faithfulness.

Now I am no longer in the world, but these are in the world, and I come to You. Holy Father, keep through Your name those whom You have given Me, that they may be one as We are. . . . I do not pray that You should take them out of the world, but that You should keep them from the evil one.

John 17:11, 15

Then Barnabas departed for Tarsus to seek Saul. And when he had found him, he brought him to Antioch. So it was that for a whole year they assembled with the church and taught a great many people. And the disciples were first called Christians in Antioch.

Acts 11:25–26

These things I write to you, though I hope to come to you shortly; but if I am delayed, I write so that you may know how you ought to conduct yourself in the house of God, which is the church of the living God, the pillar and ground of the truth.

1 Timothy 3:14–15

So continuing daily with one accord in the temple, and breaking bread from house to house, they ate their food with gladness and simplicity of heart, praising God and having favor with all the people. And the Lord added to the church daily those who were being saved.

Acts 2:46–47

THE LOCAL CHURCH is a group of believers who gather together for worship, instruction, and ministry. The body of Christ is comprised of thousands of local churches scattered over the face of the earth. The local church is not a building or an organization but a group of people, large or small, who gather together in the Lord's name. He has promised to be there in their midst. The local church is Christ's plan for winning and building believers and then sending them into the world to proclaim the gospel. That is why Satan seeks to infiltrate and undermine the local church, to weaken its witness and rob it of its power. But at the end of His earthly ministry Christ prayed for the church, that it would be united in love and delivered from the attacks of the evil one. The local church is God's idea, and no human or supernatural agency will ever be able to stamp it out. The church is alive and will continue until Christ comes back for His own.

Application: If we want to stand for Christ and resist the influence of Satan in this world, we will gather eagerly with a group of local believers, joining arms in the work of the ministry.

Response: *Father, how I praise You for the precious body of believers with whom I have the privilege to worship and serve every week.*

For those who have served well as deacons obtain for themselves a good standing and great boldness in the faith which is in Christ Jesus.

1 Timothy 3:13

For a bishop must be blameless, as a steward of God, not self-willed, not quick-tempered, not given to wine, not violent, not greedy for money, but hospitable, a lover of what is good, sober-minded, just, holy, self-controlled, holding fast the faithful word as he has been taught, that he may be able, by sound doctrine, both to exhort and convict those who contradict.

Titus 1:7–9

The elders who are among you I exhort, I who am a fellow elder and a witness of the sufferings of Christ, and also a partaker of the glory that will be revealed. Shepherd the flock of God which is among you, serving as overseers, not by constraint but willingly, not for dishonest gain but eagerly; nor as being lords over those entrusted to you, but being examples to the flock.

1 Peter 5:1–3

And He Himself gave some to be apostles, some prophets, some evangelists, and some pastors and teachers, for the equipping of the saints for the work of ministry, for the edifying of the body of Christ.

Ephesians 4:11–12

THE BIBLE RECOGNIZES two major continuing offices within the local church: deacons and elders (or bishops). Both deacons and elders are to be of the highest reputation, both within and without the church. Each is to be the husband of one wife and a good manager of his home. In general, they are to exhibit the fruits of the Spirit and not the deeds of the flesh. Deacons are to engage in works of mercy, caring for the weak, and evangelism. Those with the gift of administration are to organize and train other members of the church to do the same. Elders are to demonstrate an aptitude for teaching and to act as pastors of the flock in their care. They should be able to instruct in sound doctrine and to refute false doctrine; they should be champions of the truth of God's Word. Both deacons and elders are servants of the church, not bosses. They are called of God and have their gifts confirmed by the local church.

Application: Believers should be quick to recognize the gifts God has given to fellow believers and encourage them to answer God's call in their lives. The local church needs gifted deacons and elders.

Response: O Lord, help me to discover the gifts You have given me and to say yes when the Holy Spirit calls me to exercise those gifts in the service of the church.

Let the word of Christ dwell in you richly in all wisdom, teaching and admonishing one another in psalms and hymns and spiritual songs, singing with grace in your hearts to the Lord.

Colossians 3:16

If any believing man or woman has widows, let them relieve them, and do not let the church be burdened, that it may relieve those who are really widows.

1 Timothy 5:16

And the things that you have heard from me among many witnesses, commit these to faithful men who will be able to teach others also.

2 Timothy 2:2

Preach the word! Be ready in season and out of season. Convince, rebuke, exhort, with all longsuffering and teaching.

2 Timothy 4:2

> Having then gifts differing according to the grace that is given to us, let us use them: if prophecy, let us prophesy in proportion to our faith; or ministry, let us use it in our ministering; he who teaches, in teaching; he who exhorts, in exhortation; he who gives, with liberality; he who leads, with diligence; he who shows mercy, with cheerfulness.
>
> *Romans 12:6–8*

CHRIST IS THE HEAD of the church, and He has established its functions by precept and example. The local church represents Christ to the world and carries out the ministries He began as well as those He commanded His disciples to begin. These ministries include evangelism and missions, worship and fellowship, instruction and discipleship, service and care, governance and discipline. Included under worship and fellowship are preaching the Bible, administering the ordinances, prayer, music, and giving. All the functions and aspects of the church are related, like the systems and subsystems of a body. Some may be more public and visible, but all are essential. God has gifted various members of the church to perform these functions, and they will not be fully carried out unless all members fulfill their ministries.

Application: Believers are called not only to exercise their gifts within the church but to do so with the right spirit so that those who are ministered to may be touched by God's Spirit and come to know Christ or grow in Christ, as the case may be.

Response: Lord Jesus, it is incredible to realize that You show Your love and carry out Your ministry in the world today through individual believers in your church.

Go into all the world and preach the gospel to every creature. He who believes and is baptized will be saved; but he who does not believe will be condemned.

Mark 16:15–16

And He took bread, gave thanks and broke it, and gave it to them, saying, "This is My body which is given for you; do this in remembrance of Me." Likewise He also took the cup after supper, saying, "This cup is the new covenant in My blood, which is shed for you."

Luke 22:19–20

Or do you not know that as many of us as were baptized into Christ Jesus were baptized into His death? Therefore we were buried with Him through baptism into death, that just as Christ was raised from the dead by the glory of the Father, even so we also should walk in newness of life.

Romans 6:3–4

Then those who gladly received his word were baptized; . . . and they continued steadfastly in the apostles' doctrine and fellowship, in the breaking of bread, and in prayers.

Acts 2:41–42

DURING CHRIST'S EARTHLY ministry, He instituted two signs or ceremonies that all Christians are commanded to observe: baptism and the Lord's Supper. Both signs, or ordinances, are outward, visible representations of Christ's work of salvation and of the inward, spiritual work of grace accomplished in the hearts of all believers when they place their faith in the saving work of Christ. The Lord's Supper is a constant reminder to baptized believers of the death and resurrection of Christ on their behalf. Baptism is the sign that initiates a new believer into the fellowship of the local church. The water represents the cleansing from sin that has taken place. Repentance from sin is a prerequisite for observing both ordinances, as is faith in the saving work of Christ. Failure to observe these ordinances is disobedience to the direct commands of Christ. Failure to observe them in a serious and sober manner is to show disrespect to the work of Christ and to invite God's discipline. Proper observation of the ordinances is a source of great blessing and a means for building up one's faith.

Application: Believers must not treat baptism and partaking of the Lord's Supper as options in the Christian life. Christ designed them to be public evidences of our commitment to Him as well as needful means of growth in our faith.

Response: *Heavenly Father, may I never forget the joy of being baptized, and the blessed reminder of Christ's death on the cross when I partake in the ordinance of communion.*

THE GREAT COMMISSION

I delight to do Your will, O my God, and Your law is within my heart.

Psalm 40:8

Jesus said to them, "My food is to do the will of Him who sent Me, and to finish His work."

John 4:34

Jesus answered and said to him, "If anyone loves Me, he will keep My word; and My Father will love him, and We will come to him and make Our home with him.

John 14:23

But you shall receive power when the Holy Spirit has come upon you; and you shall be witnesses to Me in Jerusalem, and in all Judea and Samaria, and to the end of the earth.

Acts 1:8

Then Jesus came and spoke to them, saying, "All authority has been given to Me in heaven and on earth. Go therefore and make disciples of all the nations, baptizing them in the name of the Father and of the Son and of the Holy Spirit, teaching them to observe all things that I have commanded you; and lo, I am with you always, even to the end of the age."

Matthew 28:18–20

A LL BELIEVERS ARE sent by Christ into the world to be His witnesses. It is His will that we proclaim the gospel of His grace wherever we go. God's love sent Christ into the world for us, and Christ's love sends us into the world for others. For a child of God, doing what Christ says is not a matter of grudging obedience, but rather the desire of every believer's heart to please Him. It is a joyful privilege to be in Christ's service, and even to suffer for His sake. The wonder of it all is that the One who sends us goes with us, and even goes before to prepare the way!

Application: Witnessing for Christ is one of the greatest privileges of life, second only to knowing Him!

Response: Lord Jesus, I cannot believe You would choose someone like me to speak to others about You. But if You bid me go, I will go and gladly!

And He said to them, "Go into all the world and preach the gospel to every creature."

Mark 16:15

For I will not dare to speak of any of those things which Christ has not accomplished through me, in word and deed, to make the Gentiles obedient—in mighty signs and wonders, by the power of the Spirit of God, so that from Jerusalem and round about to Illyricum I have fully preached the gospel of Christ.

Romans 15:18–19

After these things I looked, and behold, a great multitude which no one could number, of all nations, tribes, peoples, and tongues, standing before the throne and before the Lamb, clothed with white robes, with palm branches in their hands.

Revelation 7:9

And this gospel of the kingdom will be preached in all the world
as a witness to all the nations, and then the end will come.

Matthew 24:14

THE SCOPE OF the Great Commission is global because God's love is global. Christ commanded His disciples to begin witnessing where they were living, in Jerusalem, but ultimately to carry the message of salvation to the ends of the earth. Christ made it clear that this message must be preached to all people before He returns to judge the world. While not every person in every people group will believe in Christ, at least one from every group must have had the opportunity. Some day individuals from every people group will stand before the throne of God with their robes washed white through the blood of Christ. The Great Commission will not be fulfilled until every human being has had the opportunity to hear a clear presentation of the gospel.

Application: Christ urges us to be involved in local evangelism, but beyond that, He wants us to do our part to evangelize the whole world.

Response: O Lord, enlarge my vision and give me a burden for the lost people of the whole world. Show me what my part in world missions should be.

For the Son of Man has come to seek and to save that which was lost.

Luke 19:10

⸎

For God so loved the world that He gave His only begotten Son, that whoever believes in Him should not perish but have everlasting life.

John 3:16

⸎

But God demonstrates His own love toward us, in that while we were still sinners, Christ died for us.

Romans 5:8

⸎

But God, who is rich in mercy, because of His great love with which He loved us, even when we were dead in trespasses, made us alive together with Christ (by grace you have been saved).

Ephesians 2:4–5

⸎

Therefore we are ambassadors for Christ, as though God were pleading through us: we implore you on Christ's behalf, be reconciled to God.

2 Corinthians 5:20

T HOUGH CHRIST HIMSELF has ordered us to preach the gospel to every human being on the face of the earth, our hearts will not be gripped by the urgency of the task until we are convinced of the hopeless, helpless condition of everyone apart from faith in Jesus Christ. Even knowing this, we will not be moved to go ourselves or to send others to go until our hearts have been arrested by the same love for lost people that sent Christ into the world. The message of the cross is a love letter from God to all who are rebelling against His rule in their lives. We are sent to love the unlovely and to wrap our arms around those who are shaking their fist in God's face in hopes that they will respond positively to His message of love.

Application: May our hearts beat for the lost with the same love and compassion that sent Christ to lay down His life for us all.

Response: Lord Jesus, inflame my heart with Your love for the lost! I did not deserve Your love, and yet You loved me anyway.

Therefore let us pursue the things which make for peace and the things by which one may edify another.

Romans 14:19

Но, speaking the truth in love, may grow up in all things into Him who is the head—Christ—from whom the whole body, joined and knit together by what every joint supplies, according to the effective working by which every part does its share, causes growth of the body for the edifying of itself in love.

Ephesians 4:15–16

Therefore comfort each other and edify one another, just as you also are doing.

1 Thessalonians 5:11

And let us consider one another in order to stir up love and good works.

Hebrews 10:24

And the things that you have heard from me among many witnesses, commit these to faithful men who will be able to teach others also.

2 Timothy 2:2

Once the lost have been reached and won to Christ, they need to become His disciples. They need to follow Him and grow to become like Him. That is why the Great Commission is not only a commandment to evangelize but a commandment to disciple. When we disciple others we teach them to be like Christ, to witness, to pray, to study the Scriptures, and to give themselves to the work of the Lord. That is why the Lord Jesus commanded us in the Great Commission to "make disciples" of all the nations, "teaching them to observe all things that I have commanded you." Not only are we called to be disciples, but we are called to encourage others to be disciples.

Application: The local church should be a place where mature Christians encourage new Christians to grow in their faith and teach them how to walk more closely to Christ.

Response: *Heavenly Father, show me how I can disciple someone to live victoriously for You.*

Most assuredly, I say to you, he who receives whomever I send receives Me; and he who receives Me receives Him who sent Me.

John 13:20

⁓⁓⁓⁓⁓

Now all things are of God, who has reconciled us to Himself through Jesus Christ, and has given us the ministry of reconciliation, that is, that God was in Christ reconciling the world to Himself, not imputing their trespasses to them, and has committed to us the word of reconciliation.

2 Corinthians 5:18–19

⁓⁓⁓⁓⁓

That I may open my mouth boldly to make known the mystery of the gospel, for which I am an ambassador in chains; that in it I may speak boldly, as I ought to speak.

Ephesians 6:20

Him we preach, warning every man and teaching every man in all
wisdom, that we may present every man perfect in Christ Jesus.

Colossians 1:28

A s WE GO INTO all the world to preach the gospel, we go as representatives of Jesus Christ. We are His ambassadors, sent out by Him to proclaim His message to a lost world. He has authorized us to declare His will and the forgiveness of sins He came to provide. As His disciples, we are expected to walk in His steps and to live in accordance with His will. If we represent our Master well, others will be drawn to Him. If we do not, we may become an obstacle to the faith of others. As Christians, our mission is to preach, teach, and reach others for Jesus Christ. Our mission will not be complete until the last person is won to Christ. God Himself will conclude the mission and call His ambassadors home. Until then, we are to pray and stay on mission.

Application: Christopher Columbus, whose first name means "Christ-bearer," considered himself to be on a mission to carry the gospel to the new world. He not only planted the flag of the King of Spain when he landed in the West Indies, but the cross of Jesus Christ.

Response: Lord Jesus, I rejoice in the privilege of serving You and in the knowledge that You not only send me to tell others about salvation, but You accompany me as I go.

PRAYER

⟪∾∾∾∾∾⟫

Prayer

Give unto the LORD the glory due to His name; worship the
LORD in the beauty of holiness.

Psalm 29:2

Bless the LORD, O my soul!
O LORD my God, You are very great:
You are clothed with honor and majesty.

Psalm 104:1

Blessed be the name of the LORD
From this time forth and forevermore!
From the rising of the sun to its going down
The LORD's name is to be praised.

Psalm 113:2–3

In this manner, therefore, pray, "Our Father in heaven,
hallowed be Your name."

Matthew 6:9

And all the angels stood around the throne and the elders and the four living creatures, and fell on their faces before the throne and worshiped God, saying: "Amen! Blessing and glory and wisdom, thanksgiving and honor and power and might, be to our God forever and ever. Amen."

Revelation 7:11–12

ORDINARILY, WE THINK of prayer as asking God for something. But our requests will never have the boldness or the appropriateness they should have unless we have spent time first in adoration of God. One cannot be in the presence of God and not bow before Him in praise and adoration. Praise is pure worship. Whereas thanksgiving is the believer's response to God for what He has done, praise is the believer's response to God for who He is.

We are creatures, and praise is the creature's response to the Creator. As Creator, God alone is worthy of adoration. To worship anything or anyone else is idolatry. While human beings may refuse to adore Jesus Christ today, one day every knee shall bow. The irony is that we never rise so high as when we are on our face before the Lord. Worship lifts and ennobles us because it demonstrates that we are made in the image of God—made for worship and a personal relationship with our Creator.

Application: A wonderful guide to a time of praise and adoration is found in the book of Psalms. There, the psalmist blesses the Lord for His incredible attributes and His mighty works.

Response: Heavenly Father, I adore You more than life itself! Your holy presence is the most important thing in my life.

I acknowledged my sin to You,
And my iniquity I have not hidden.
I said, "I will confess my transgressions to the LORD,
And You forgave the iniquity of my sin."

Psalm 32:5

Wash me thoroughly from my iniquity,
And cleanse me from my sin.
For I acknowledge my transgressions,
And my sin is always before me.

Psalm 51:2–3

And forgive us our sins, for we also forgive everyone who
is indebted to us. And do not lead us into temptation, but
deliver us from the evil one.

Luke 11:4

Confession

> If we confess our sins, He is faithful and just to forgive us our sins and to cleanse us from all unrighteousness.
>
> *1 John 1:9*

WHEN WE COME to Christ in repentance and receive him as Savior, we are cleansed of our sins completely. Thereafter, when we sin, it is like an ancient traveler whose feet are dirty from walking on dusty roads in open sandals. When the traveler comes in off the road, he just needs to have his feet washed to be completely clean again. When we confess the particular sins we have committed since the last time we confessed, God declares us forgiven and completely cleansed from all unrighteousness. The effects of unconfessed and unforsaken sin for the believer are far more serious than unwashed feet! Since God made us to have fellowship with Him, any sin in our lives has the effect of breaking fellowship, though not the relationship, between us and our heavenly Father. We need to confess our sin to God, forsake it, receive His forgiveness, and serve Him again.

Application: As believers we must lead the way in calling moral offenses what they really are: sin, an offense against the holiness of God, the moral law-giver of the universe.

Response: O Lord, You know the thoughts and intents of my heart. I ask You to forgive me and cleanse me from those sinful thoughts and actions that Your Holy Spirit is pointing out to me even now.

Prayer

Bless the LORD, O my soul;
And all that is within me, bless His holy name!
Bless the LORD, O my soul,
And forget not all His benefits.

Psalm 103:1–2

So Jesus answered and said, "Were there not ten cleansed? But where are the nine? Were there not any found who returned to give glory to God except this foreigner?"

Luke 17:17–18

Giving thanks always for all things to God the Father in the name of our Lord Jesus Christ.

Ephesians 5:20

Every good gift and every perfect gift is from above, and comes down from the Father of lights, with whom there is no variation or shadow of turning.

James 1:17

In everything give thanks; for this is the will of God in Christ
Jesus for you.

1 Thessalonians 5:18

WHEN SOMEONE RECEIVES a gift, the most natural thing—indeed
the expected thing—is to express gratitude to the giver. Perhaps
that is why the Lord expressed disappointment when only one out of
ten lepers whom He cleansed bothered to return to give thanks. The
believer knows where his or her blessings come from! In fact, when any
good thing happens to Christians, the spontaneous response of their
hearts is to exult: "Thank you, Lord!" But for the unbeliever, the greatest tragedy is to experience something special and have no one to
thank. Perhaps the most distinctive thing about a believer's gratitude is
that it is possible to be thankful even in difficult circumstances. By
God's grace we learn to give thanks in every circumstance.

Application: There is so much we can thank God for: life, health, loved
ones, meaningful work, yes, even hard circumstances. Most of all, we
can be thankful for our salvation and the grace in which we stand.

*Response: Where do I begin to thank You, Father, for all you have done
for me? My heart is so full, but I want to start by thanking you for the Lord
Jesus Christ and the eternal life He purchased for me on the cross.*

I do not pray for these alone, but also for those who will believe in Me through their word; that they all may be one as You, Father, are in Me, and I in You; that they also may be one in Us, that the world may believe that You sent Me.

John 17:20–21

ಯಯ

Peter was therefore kept in prison, but constant prayer was offered to God for him by the church. Now behold, an angel of the Lord stood by him, and a light shone in the prison, and he struck Peter on the side and raised him up, saying, "Arise quickly!" And his chains fell off his hands.

Acts 12:5, 7

ಯಯ

Likewise the Spirit also helps in our weaknesses. For we do not know what we should pray for as we ought, but the Spirit Himself makes intercession for us with groanings which cannot be uttered.

Romans 8:26

Therefore I exhort first of all that supplications, prayers, intercessions, and giving of thanks be made for all men, for kings and all who are in authority, that we may lead a quiet and peaceable life in all godliness and reverence.

1 Timothy 2:1–2

A SPECIAL FORM of prayer or supplication is prayer on behalf of others. Aside from praise and adoration of God Himself, there is no nobler type of prayer than to intercede before God on behalf of the needs of others. In the Old Testament, this was a special responsibility of prophets and priests, and before them of the patriarchs. In the New Testament, the responsibility for intercessory prayer is extended to all believers. We are commanded to pray for one another and for leadership at all levels, both within the church and in the government. We are to pray for the sick that they might be healed, for the lost that they might be saved, and for the saved that they might grow in their faith. In it all, we are to pray that God might receive the glory for answers to our prayers.

Application: If we write down our prayers requests on behalf of others, and later record the answers to our prayers, we will have a permanent record of the work of God in our lives and through us in the lives of others.

Response: Father, may I be found faithful in praying for others in need. They are depending on me, just as I am on You.

I have been young, and now am old;
Yet I have not seen the righteous forsaken,
Nor his descendants begging bread.

Psalm 37:25

Your kingdom come. Your will be done on earth as it is in heaven. Give us this day our daily bread.

Matthew 6:10–11

Ask, and it will be given to you; seek, and you will find; knock, and it will be opened to you. For everyone who asks receives, and he who seeks finds, and to him who knocks it will be opened.

Matthew 7:7–8

And my God shall supply all your need according to His riches in glory by Christ Jesus.

Philippians 4:19

But seek first the kingdom of God and His righteousness, and all
these things shall be added to you.

Matthew 6:33

A PRAYER OF petition is asking God persistently in faith for the right
thing with the right motive. Supplication is asking with a sense of
urgency. When we come to God with our petitions, it should never be
casually or indifferently. Our whole heart and soul should be poured
out before God in earnest prayer. Supplication includes all personal
petitions, all requests for God to meet our personal needs. It was with
this large category of prayer in mind that Jesus taught His disciples to
pray for daily bread. God wants to be involved in the everyday details
of our lives. He wants us to come to Him with every need. Why?
Because He loves us and delights to demonstrate His love by supplying
our every need.

Application: To receive God's provision for all of our needs, we must
ask in faith believing.

*Response: O God, as I present my petitions to You, I ask that Your perfect
will be done in my life. I know You will provide everything that I need so
I can bring glory to You.*

WORSHIP

And I prayed to the L<small>ORD</small> my God, and made confession, and said, "O Lord, great and awesome God, who keeps His covenant and mercy with those who love Him, and with those who keep His commandments, we have sinned and committed iniquity, we have done wickedly and rebelled, even by departing from Your precepts and Your judgments."

Daniel 9:4–5

And when they had prayed, the place where they were assembled together was shaken; and they were all filled with the Holy Spirit, and they spoke the word of God with boldness.

Acts 4:31

And having a High Priest over the house of God, let us draw near with a true heart in full assurance of faith, having our hearts sprinkled from an evil conscience and our bodies washed with pure water . . . not forsaking the assembling of ourselves together, as is the manner of some, but exhorting one another, and so much the more as you see the Day approaching.

Hebrews 10:21–22, 25

Praise

If My people who are called by My name will humble themselves,
and pray and seek My face, and turn from their wicked ways, then I
will hear from heaven, and will forgive their sin and heal their land.

2 Chronicles 7:14

THE MOST POWERFUL thing that a body of believers can do together is
to worship and praise God. God inhabits the praises of His people,
and He responds to the prayers of His people. When true revival comes
to a church or a community, it does not affect just a few individuals here
and there. Rather, it sweeps across whole congregations and whole com-
munities, sometimes crossing national and international boundaries.
When God's people are united in worship and prayer, revival breaks
out. Clearly, it is because there is shared conviction over sin and a
shared burden to experience God's grace and mercy. When the prayer
meeting is the most neglected meeting of the church, there is no foundation for the Holy Spirit to do His unique work of bringing revival to
God's people. By contrast, when God's people humble themselves and
beg for His mercy, God opens the windows of heaven, and pours out
floods of blessing.

Application: The most practical step we can take that will allow the
Holy Spirit to do His sovereign work of producing revival is to examine
our lives for all known sin, confess and forsake it, and attend the prayer
meetings of the church faithfully. As we join with other believers in
praise and prayer to our God, He will surely act just as He has promised.

*Response: Holy Spirit, give me a fresh vision of the holiness of God and
convict me of sin, righteousness and judgment. I desire Your sovereign
touch on my life and the life of my church.*

He has put a new song in my mouth—
Praise to our God;
Many will see it and fear,
And will trust in the LORD.

Psalm 40:3

He has put a new song in my mouth—

My lips shall greatly rejoice when I sing to You,
And my soul, which You have redeemed.

Psalm 71:23

I will sing of the mercies of the LORD forever;
With my mouth will I make known Your faithfulness to all
generations.

Psalm 89:1

And do not be drunk with wine, in which is dissipation;
but be filled with the Spirit, speaking to one another in
psalms and hymns and spiritual songs, singing and making
melody in your heart to the Lord, giving thanks always for
all things to God the Father in the name of our Lord Jesus
Christ.

Ephesians 5:18–20

Let the word of Christ dwell in you richly in all wisdom, teaching and admonishing one another in psalms and hymns and spiritual songs, singing with grace in your hearts to the Lord.

Colossians 3:16

IN ADDITION TO praying, believers worship and praise God through music, particularly in singing hymns. It is striking that God's people, the people of the Bible, express their joy and love for God in this fashion. Music is a powerful medium for teaching as well as for voicing praise to God. Because of the poetic form of most hymns, they are also a tremendous aid in remembering spiritual truths.

While singing may be a spontaneous expression of the heart for individual believers, it is commanded as part of corporate worship both in the Old and New Testaments. And, as the book of Revelation makes clear, it is and will be part of corporate worship in heaven. The early church developed songs that proclaimed the gospel and gave praise to the Trinity. Over the centuries, the church has continued to compose and sing new hymns of the faith as part of its corporate worship.

Application: Today some believers prefer to sing short praise choruses, while others enjoy the classic hymns of the faith. Both can bring honor and glory to God when sung with a heart of thanksgiving.

Response: Heavenly Father, how I love to sing praises to Your name! And how I need to be instructed by the hymns of the faith.

But the Helper, the Holy Spirit, whom the Father will send in My name, He will teach you all things, and bring to your remembrance all things that I said to you.

John 14:26

So then faith comes by hearing, and hearing by the word of God.

Romans 10:17

For this reason we also thank God without ceasing, because when you received the word of God which you heard from us, you welcomed it not as the word of men, but as it is in truth, the word of God, which also effectively works in you who believe.

1 Thessalonians 2:13

For the word of God is living and powerful, and sharper than any two-edged sword, piercing even to the division of soul and spirit, and of joints and marrow, and is a discerner of the thoughts and intents of the heart.

Hebrews 4:12

All Scripture is given by inspiration of God, and is profitable for doctrine, for reproof, for correction, for instruction in righteousness, that the man of God may be complete, thoroughly equipped for every good work.

2 Timothy 3:16

THE CENTERPIECE OF every worship service is the preaching and teaching of God's Word. Faith comes by hearing, and hearing by the Word of God. For people to come to Christ and to grow in their faith, they must hear the Word. All Scripture is inspired by God and is profitable for learning doctrine, for reproving sin and correcting the sinner, and for instructing believers in righteous living. Teaching God's Word in the church is a vital ministry, but daily personal Bible study outside of worship services is also important for our spiritual well-being. Meditating upon passages of Scripture and even memorizing them are additional ways we can internalize the Word of God. The important thing is not only to hear but to do the Word of God. We are saved and we mature in the Christian faith by hearing and obeying God's holy Word.

Application: There are many study resources available to help us gain added insights into God's Word. Some of these include concordances, dictionaries, encyclopedias, and atlases.

Response: *O God, I pray that the Holy Spirit will illumine the pages of Scripture as I study Your Word. He inspired the original writers, and I want Him to be my Teacher today.*

Therefore if you bring your gift to the altar, and there remember that your brother has something against you, leave your gift there before the altar, and go your way. First be reconciled to your brother, and then come and offer your gift.

Matthew 5:23–24

A new commandment I give to you, that you love one another; as I have loved you, that you also love one another. By this all will know that you are My disciples, if you have love for one another.

John 13:34–35

Therefore if there is any consolation in Christ, if any comfort of love, if any fellowship of the Spirit, if any affection and mercy, fulfill my joy by being likeminded, having the same love, being of one accord, of one mind.

Philippians 2:1–2

If we say that we have fellowship with Him, and walk in darkness, we lie and do not practice the truth. But if we walk in the light as He is in the light, we have fellowship with one another, and the blood of Jesus Christ His Son cleanses us from all sin.

1 John 1:6–7

THE LORD JESUS' final prayer for His disciples while here upon the earth was that they become one. He had earlier given them a new commandment that they should love one another as He had loved them. That love, the love of Christ, is what grips the hearts of believers and binds them to other believers. It is what creates a fellowship of believers. We can have fellowship with others whom we have just met for the first time because we belong to a common spiritual family: we are brothers and sisters in Jesus Christ. In fact, we can feel closer to them than we do to long-standing acquaintances, or even friends, who are not believers.

Application: It is important that we let nothing interrupt the fellowship we have with the Lord and with other believers. At the end of each day let us determine whether we harbor any unconfessed sin or hard feelings toward a fellow believer.

Response: Father, I ask You to search my heart and show me any sin or resentment lurking there toward fellow believers.

His lord said to him, "Well done, good and faithful servant; you were faithful over a few things, I will make you ruler over many things. Enter into the joy of your lord."

Matthew 25:21

If anyone serves Me, let him follow Me; and where I am, there My servant will be also. If anyone serves Me, him My Father will honor.

John 12:26

I beseech you therefore, brethren, by the mercies of God, that you present your bodies a living sacrifice, holy, acceptable to God, which is your reasonable service.

Romans 12:1

For though I am free from all men, I have made myself a servant to all, that I might win the more.

1 Corinthians 9:19

And whoever desires to be first among you, let him be your slave—just as the Son of Man did not come to be served, but to serve, and to give His life a ransom for many.

Matthew 20:27–28

FOR THE CHRISTIAN, service to God and to others is part of worship. The Lord Jesus set the example for us to follow, declaring that He had come into the world not to be served, but to serve and to give His life as a ransom for many. On more than one occasion, He had to remind His disciples that their notion of leadership, which was to have positions of preeminence, power, and authority over others, was exactly the opposite of God's notion. A servant is not greater than his master, and our Master set an example that we are to follow. For that reason, Paul declares himself to be a bondservant of Jesus Christ and a servant to the churches he founded, as Peter, James, and Jude also do. For the believer, service to others is always provided in the name of Christ so that at the end of the age we may hear Him declare to us, "Well done, good and faithful servant."

Application: In many churches, it is difficult to find believers who are willing to serve the needs of the church. How refreshing it would be if church members volunteered to serve even before they were asked.

Response: Lord Jesus, You showed what it means to be a servant when You gave Your life for me. May I demonstrate the same spirit of service when I am called upon to minister to others.

LAST THINGS

When the Son of Man comes in His glory, and all the holy angels with Him, then He will sit on the throne of His glory. All the nations will be gathered before Him, and He will separate them one from another, as a shepherd divides his sheep from the goats.

Matthew 25:31–32

Jesus said to him, "It is as you said. Nevertheless, I say to you, hereafter you will see the Son of Man sitting at the right hand of the Power, and coming on the clouds of heaven."

Matthew 26:64

But of that day and hour no one knows, neither the angels in heaven, nor the Son, but only the Father.

Mark 13:32

But concerning the times and the seasons, brethren, you have no need that I should write to you. For you yourselves know perfectly that the day of the Lord so comes as a thief in the night.

1 Thessalonians 5:1–2

For the Lord Himself will descend from heaven with a shout,
with the voice of an archangel, and with the trumpet of God.

1 Thessalonians 4:16

WHILE BIBLE-BELIEVING Christians may differ on matters such as the rapture, the tribulation, the millennial kingdom, the timing of the judgment, and the eternal kingdom, all agree on the certainty of Christ's second coming. Jesus is coming back again suddenly in great power and glory. And when He does, every eye shall see Him and every knee shall bow before Him. When Jesus returns, accompanied by the holy angels, He will bring the spirits of those who have died in Christ with Him. Their bodies will be raised first, and then those believers who are alive will have their bodies transformed into new resurrection bodies just like Jesus' body. All believers will be caught up into the sky to meet the Lord in the air and will be forever with Him. The return of Jesus Christ to defeat His enemies and establish His kingdom is a blessed hope of the believer.

Application: As believers we can rest assured that one day Christ will suddenly break through the sky and return for His own. This gives us confidence in the ultimate victory of the Lord over all the effects of evil in this world, including sin, suffering, and death.

Response: *Dear Lord Jesus, my heart beats faster just at the thought of Your triumphant return! How I look forward to that day!*

For the Son of Man will come in the glory of His Father with His angels, and then He will reward each according to his works.

Matthew 16:27

So then each of us shall give account of himself to God. Therefore let us not judge one another anymore, but rather resolve this, not to put a stumbling block or a cause to fall in our brother's way.

Romans 14:12–13

And whatever you do, do it heartily, as to the Lord and not to men, knowing that from the Lord you will receive the reward of the inheritance; for you serve the Lord Christ.

Colossians 3:23–24

And behold, I am coming quickly, and My reward is with Me, to give to every one according to his work.

Revelation 22:12

> Therefore we make it our aim, whether present or absent, to be well pleasing to Him. For we must all appear before the judgment seat of Christ, that each one may receive the things done in the body, according to what He has done, whether good or bad.
>
> *2 Corinthians 5:9–10*

WHEN CHRIST RETURNS to judge the world, all believers will stand before Him to have their lives evaluated and to receive rewards for faithful service. As believers, we do not face a final condemning judgment for our sins because the Lord Jesus took that judgment on the cross. But we will be examined for our faithfulness as stewards of what the Lord has placed in our hands. Our lives as Christians count, and the rewards we will gain or lose are opportunities for service in the kingdom. Each time Jesus sees something we did in thought, word, or action that was an act of obedience done out of faith, He will commend us. What a joy it will be to be found faithful, and to hear our Lord Jesus say to us, "Well done, good and faithful servant. Enter into the joy of your Lord."

Application: As Christians, future rewards should not be our chief concern, but rather how much we can please and help others to please the Lord we love with all of our hearts.

Response: Lord Jesus, I know I shall stand before You one day to have You examine my life. I want You to be pleased with the quality of my life.

And being in torment in Hades, he lifted up his eyes and saw Abraham afar off, and Lazarus in his bosom. Then he cried and said, "Father Abraham, have mercy on me, and send Lazarus that he may dip the tip of his finger in water and cool my tongue; for I am tormented in this flame."

Luke 16:23–24

So it will be at the end of the age. The angels will come forth, separate the wicked from among the just, and cast them into the furnace of fire. There will be wailing and gnashing of teeth.

Matthew 13:49–50

Then He will also say to those on the left hand, "Depart from Me, you cursed, into the everlasting fire prepared for the devil and his angels." . . . And these will go away into everlasting punishment, but the righteous into eternal life.

Matthew 25:41, 46

And anyone not found written in the Book of Life was cast into the lake of fire.

Revelation 20:15

> He who believes in Him is not condemned; but he who does not believe is condemned already, because he has not believed in the name of the only begotten Son of God.
>
> *John 3:18*

THE BIBLE TEACHES that those who persist in hardening their hearts toward God and do not accept His Son as their Savior, will one day face Jesus Christ as their Judge and be held accountable for what they have done in this life. At the beginning of the human race, God made it clear that death, both spiritual and physical, was the ultimate consequence of rebelling against Him and disbelieving His Word. All people begin spiritually dead, with no desire for God or His Word. And they stay that way, in active rebellion against the light they have, until God in His mercy intervenes and brings them to life. Just as there are degrees of reward, so there are degrees of punishment based on the light we have and the choices we make. We do not know what the conscious experience of hell will be like, but we do know from Jesus' story of the rich man and Lazarus in the Bible that it will entail torment and separation from the presence of God. It will be lonely and completely dark. And it will be eternal.

Application: The love of Christ should constrain us to bring the saving message of the gospel to a lost world. Let us warn everyone to avoid eternity without God.

Response: O Father, I have to admit my coldness of heart toward those outside of Christ. Ignite my heart with the same compassion You showed to me!

Watch therefore, for you know neither the day nor the hour in which the Son of Man is coming.

Matthew 25:13

But you, brethren, are not in darkness, so that this Day should overtake you as a thief. Therefore let us not sleep, as others do, but let us watch and be sober.

1 Thessalonians 5:4, 6

Looking for the blessed hope and glorious appearing of our great God and Savior Jesus Christ.

Titus 2:13

But the end of all things is at hand; therefore be serious and watchful in your prayers.

1 Peter 4:7

And now, little children, abide in Him, that when He appears, we may have confidence and not be ashamed before Him at His coming.

1 John 2:28

Beloved, now we are children of God; and it has not yet been revealed what we shall be, but we know that when He is revealed, we shall be like Him, for we shall see Him as He is. And everyone who has this hope in Him purifies himself, just as He is pure.

1 John 3:2–3

THE MAJOR REASON the Lord Jesus shared the events and signs of His second coming was so that those who were going to be alive at the time of His return would know that His coming was near. Even more importantly, it was intended to make them alert, watchful, and expectant. The Lord wanted His people to be ready for His return. Readiness consists primarily in having one's life in order and being busy doing the Master's work. In this way, a person need not be ashamed if Jesus should suddenly appear. Whether one is alive when Christ returns or goes home to be with Him prior to His return, a believer should lead a godly life. In fact, the expectation of His soon return should be the greatest motivator for godly living.

Application: The only way to be prepared for Christ's return is to discipline one's life by spending time each day reading God's Word and praying. Each day should begin and end in the Lord's presence, asking Him to search our hearts and minds.

Response: O Lord, I wear the label of the risen Savior and desire to live a pure and godly life so He will not be ashamed of me when He comes.

Whatever your hand finds to do, do it with your might; for there is no work or device or knowledge or wisdom in the grave where you are going.

Ecclesiastes 9:10

Who then is a faithful and wise servant, whom his master made ruler over his household, to give them food in due season? Blessed is that servant whom his master, when he comes, will find so doing.

Matthew 24:45–46

But none of these things move me; nor do I count my life dear to myself, so that I may finish my race with joy, and the ministry which I received from the Lord Jesus, to testify to the gospel of the grace of God.

Acts 20:24

And whatever you do, do it heartily, as to the Lord and not to men.

Colossians 3:23

Do business till I come.

Luke 19:13

WE ARE TO BE OCCUPIED with the Lord's business until He comes. Moreover, we are stewards of the Lord's resources and will be held accountable for our stewardship when He returns. As stewards, we are to be found faithful in carrying out our assignment, the business the Lord has given us to do. The Lord's business, given to us in the Great Commission, is to seek and to save those who are lost and to equip those who are saved to do the work of the ministry. The specific business God has called us to do will depend on the gifts, talents, and opportunities He has given us. Our assignment includes the work, or vocation, to which He has called us and through which we are to shine as lights in a dark world. Both in our jobs and in our lives, we are to be living letters from the Lord that everyone can read. Through our work and our words, we are to be witnesses for the Lord Jesus Christ.

Application: Like the Lord Jesus when He was in the temple at twelve years of age, we must be about our Father's business. We must apply ourselves and redeem the time, all the more as we see the day of Christ's return approaching.

Response: *O Lord, You exemplified a life of diligence here on earth. Help me to be diligent and watchful until You return.*